The Church in Quebec

Gregory Baum

The Church in Quebec

NOVALIS

Cover design and layout: Gilles Lépine

© 1991 Novalis, Saint Paul University, Ottawa

Business Office: Novalis, P.O. Box 990, Outremont, P.Q. H2V 4S7

Legal Deposit: 2nd trimester 1991
 National Library of Canada
 Bibliothèque nationale du Québec

ISBN 2-89088-487-2

Printed in Canada

Canadian Cataloguing in Publication Data

   Baum, Gregory, 1923-

   The Church in Quebec

   Includes bibliographical references and index.

   ISBN 2-89088-497-2

   1. Catholic Church — Quebec (Province) — History. 2.
Religion and culture — Quebec (Province). 3. Nationalism
— Quebec (Province) — Religious aspects — Catholic
Church. 4. Quebec (Province) — Church history. I. Title.

BX1422.Q8B38 1991   282'-714   C91-096492-0

NOVALIS

Contents

Foreword

Un Québécois d'adoption is what Gregory Baum has become. Living in Montreal and working in an anglophone environment, Gregory Baum is well placed to travel between the two proverbial "solitudes," and Montreal is the fortunate beneficiary of his shift from Toronto. Convivial and gregarious, he has made numerous friends through the various groups in which he is active: the Catholic left, the Polanyi Institute, the New Democratic Party, the McGill University environment. I feel most privileged to be included amongst these friends. Perhaps the generation of students who hear his views on social ethics at a time when all values are being questioned and challenged will profit most from his move to Quebec.

Not only does he observe and participate in Quebec society, but he has made it his duty, his mission almost, to dispel prejudice and ignorance, to explain Quebec to Canada. Running through the articles published in this book is a complaint — Canada neither knows nor understands Quebec's culture, politics or religion.

As a person actively participating in the world around him, Gregory Baum never ceases to assess this world critically. What we have in these articles is not the detached gaze of the outside observer but the engaged analysis of the theologian and the sociologist, endowed with what his wife Shirley refers to as his "dialectical mind," and propelled by a sympathetic understanding of the people and the milieu he has chosen to study. His background in theology and sociology and his commitment as a progressive Catholic and socialist make him more than a commentator and a critic; he is an interpreter, sometimes a popularizer but always an engaged analyst.

In this post-Meech Lake era, in the midst of an economic depression, when our leaders envisage cutting social services while the country is further indebted by its embroilment in a distant war, we have here someone who does not lose sight of the broad issues. When discussing contemporary issues with him, it becomes clear that nothing is taken for granted, that no observation is gratuitous and that his judgment is guided by his vision of social justice. "From the bottom and from the margin" is a phrase I immediately associate with him. He has wholeheartedly endorsed the church's "option for the poor," the perspective that colours his views on Quebec society.

This collection of Gregory Baum's articles will prove invaluable for English-speaking Canadians who seek a better understanding of Quebec and, particularly, of the church in Quebec. In Chapter One he turns to an historical account of the process of secularization since the Quiet Revolution. In his well-known book, *Catholics and Canadian Socialism*, he charts the church's march toward pluralism over the last forty years. Similarly, his second chapter on the Dumont Report stresses the democratizing of the Quebec church.

In Chapters Three, Four and Five Baum introduces his readers to the Christian socialists of the seventies, theologian Jacques Grand'Maison, another Catholic who opted for those at the bottom, and Douglas Hall, a

Protestant known internationally for his contextual theology.

In his last two essays Baum tackles head on the most controversial, and to many anglophones unacceptable, questions in Quebec today: the language legislation and nationalism up to and including separation. He has tried to understand Quebec nationalism from the inside. He has developed his empathy by meeting Quebec nationalists, by reading their works, by going out of his way to establish contacts and to listen. He sets in historical context the debate surrounding the passing of bills 101 and 178 and approaches the issue from the perspective of collective rights as redress to historical wrongs.

Church attendance by Catholics is so low nowadays, especially in large urban centres, that one might be tempted to conclude that the church has become irrelevant. Yet, in Chapter Seven Baum presents a church whose bishops are actively taking part in one of today's major social questions: Quebec nationalism.

Gregory Baum could have chosen to present any aspect of Quebec society to an anglophone audience. He has selected that which he knows most intimately, the church. It should reach a receptive ear. After all was not the church generally portrayed as the main culprit for Quebec's backwardness, right-wing nationalism, even fascist tendencies? That church is gone in Quebec today; only vestiges remain. (A trip to Gaspé with Shirley and Gregory has shown me how sensitive he is to these vestiges evident in the country churches and the prominent monuments.) Despite the erosion of its former prestige and influence, the church remains a credible commentator on social and economic questions ranging from unemployment to ethnic relations.

Resisting a post-modern *fin de siècle* too easily dismissive of universal values and collective rights, Gregory Baum stresses ethics and social justice. This book takes the reader back to basics. It asks fundamental questions while explaining a society and one of its traditional institutions. Most importantly the articles contained here will contribute to a better understanding of recent developments in Quebec and prepare Canadian readers for the new Quebec evolving and transforming itself in the nineteen-nineties.

Andrée Lévesque
Department of History
McGill University

Preface

In the fall of 1986 I moved to Montreal. After teaching at St. Michael's College in the University of Toronto for a period of twenty-seven years, I became professor of religious studies at McGill University. This was not my first time in Quebec. In 1977 I had taught one term at McGill University. A few years later, thanks to an exchange program between the religious studies department of the University of Toronto and the equivalent department of the University of Quebec in Montreal (UQAM), I became a visiting professor at that university in the 1981-82 academic year. It was only when I moved permanently to Montreal in 1986 that I had the opportunity to enter more deeply into the life of Quebec society.

How I became an active participant in the francophone society deserves an explanation. The academic life at McGill University is conducted in English. The same is true of Concordia University. There is in Montreal an entire community — with its universities, schools, hospitals, theatres and social agencies — that uses English to communicate. It is therefore possible for a professor to move from Toronto to Montreal without ever learning French and gaining access to the intellectual life, culture and political debates of the French-speaking majority.

My case was distinct because as a Catholic theologian I was welcomed with open arms by the progressive wing of the Catholic church. The Jesuit-sponsored monthly, *Relations*, a critical review dealing with culture, politics and religion, asked me to join its editorial committee. I accepted the invitation with gratitude. The discussions at our regular meetings, dealing with the policy of the review and the content of the monthly issues, introduced me to the topics and problems debated in Quebec society. Every month *Relations* organizes for its readers and their friends a *soirée*, an evening session to examine an important contemporary issue: brief statements made by three or four panelists are followed by a discussion involving all participants. Every other summer *Relations* organizes a four-day colloquium on issues important in Quebec, following the same method of panel discussion and audience participation. In addition to this, what has helped me to become an active member of Quebec society is my membership in several other religious and secular associations. All of this I regard as a privilege and an adventure.

When I taught for a year at the University of Quebec in Montreal in 1981, I realized that without a knowledge of Quebec history and an understanding of the Quiet Revolution it was impossible to interpret the debates taking place in society or the pastoral policies adopted by the Catholic church. A book I found very helpful in my studies was *Quebec: Social Change and Political Crisis*, written by two Toronto professors, Dale Posgate and Kenneth McRoberts. Of particular interest to me was a better understanding of the Quiet Revolution's impact on the Catholic church. The article I wrote on that occasion, "Catholicism and Secularization in Quebec," sought to clarify the destabilizing as well as the vivifying impact of the Quiet Revolution on the believing community of Catholics. The article, published in the American quarterly *Cross Currents* 36 (Winter 1986-87), is the first chapter of this collection.

The present book is not a systematic study of the church in Quebec. It is a collection of articles I wrote on events, persons and topics related to the Quebec church, which I found particularly interesting. These articles have been published, in English or in French, in journals of various kinds. Chapter Two, "The Dumont Report: Democratizing the Catholic Church," appears in *Sociologie et société* (October 1990), published by the University of Montreal. Chapter Three, "*Politisés chrétiens:* A Christian-Marxist Network in Quebec, 1974-1982," was printed in *Studies in Political Economy* (Summer 1990). Chapter Four, "Jacques Grand'Maison: Prophecy and Politics," was a paper given at a conference on this important socio-theological thinker, sponsored by the theological faculty of the University of Montreal. The paper was later published in the Confer ence proceedings, under the title *Crise de prophétisme hier et aujourd'hui* (Montreal: Fides, 1990). Chapter Five, "Douglas Hall: Contextual Theology," was written to introduce the thought of my colleague, an English-speaking Protestant theologian, to the French-speaking theological community. The piece was published in the *Laval théologique et philosophique* 46 (June 1990) of Laval University, Quebec City. Chapter Six, "Ethical Reflections on the Quebec Language Debate," is the slightly edited version of an article that appeared in *Catholic New Times* (March 5, 1989). Included in this chapter are ideas I developed in the piece "Reflections after a Long Lunch," published in the Montreal Social Justice Committee's newsletter *Upstream Journal* (February 1989). Chapter Seven, "The Bishops and Quebec Nationalism," appeared in *Arc* (Spring 1989), published by the McGill faculty of religious studies.

The reason why I thought it worthwhile to publish these articles as a book was not simply because I personally found the topics very exciting but also and more especially because there is very little literature in English dealing with issues of church and society in Quebec. I always regret that the Catholic theological literature of Quebec is almost unknown by Catholic theologians in English-speaking Canada. I hope to write on Quebec theology in the future. The present book leaves out many topics related to church and society, among them the reaction of the Christian churches in Quebec to the self-affirmation of the Native peoples, and in particular to the protest of the Mohawk nation in 1990.

I wish to express my gratitude to many friends and colleagues at the McGill faculty of religious studies, at the editorial committee of *Relations*, at Club jeudi of Montreal's Karl Polanyi Institute, at the collective La théologie contextuelle, at the Centre Saint-Pierre and the Ligue des droits et libertés. I also wish to thank Novalis for its gracious co-operation. Thanks also go to my wife, Shirley, who does not resent the long hours I spend in front of my word processor.

Gregory Baum
December 13, 1990

Chapter One

Catholicism and Secularization in Quebec

Quebec culture and religion are not well-known in English-speaking North America. In this essay I analyse the entry of Quebec Catholicism into the modern age. I shall first present an historical account of what is known as the Quiet Revolution; then I shall examine a theory of the British sociologist, David Martin, that sheds light on the process of secularization. Finally I shall propose a twofold thesis regarding religion and modernization in Quebec.

The Old Quebec and the Quiet Revolution

Quebec, though a province in the 1867 Canadian confederation, *n'est pas une province comme les autres.* It is the heartland of French culture in North America, heir of a vital tradition derived from *la Nouvelle-France,* the old French colony on the banks of the St. Lawrence River. French Canadians think of themselves as a people. They "constitute a linguistic and cultural group with roots three centuries old in the soil of Canada, the soil which has served them as 'the cradle of their life, labour, sorrow and dreams,' a group of people vividly aware that they make up a community enjoying a unity, individuality and spirit of their own, all of which yield them an unshakable right to their own existence and development."[1] In brief, French Canadians regard themselves as a nation and consider Canada a binational political entity.

After the 1763 British conquest, a few years prior to the American Revolution, the British Crown wanted Quebec to be a peaceful and loyal colony. The Crown was willing to guarantee the rights of the Catholic church if the bishops promised to pacify the population. The bishops consented. They were grateful for receiving royal recognition. After the failed rebellion of 1837, the bishops again helped to pacify the colony. In the 1840s, thanks to a new, ultramontane Catholicism — aggressive, disciplined and other-worldly, promoted by a large number of priests and religious arriving from France — the Catholic church was able to affirm itself as the spiritual and cultural force that defined, with ever-increasing intensity, the social reality of French Canada. This Catholicism was the religious cement that enabled French Canadians to resist assimilation and decline. They remained a vital people.

In 1867 the bishops gave their consent, with Pope Pius IX's approval, to the new Canadian confederation. They hoped that this new political arrangement would assure the identity, vitality and freedom of *le peuple canadien*. The church remained the soul of the people. It taught them to pray and believe in eternal life, it educated them, it made them into dedicated workers on the land and in the bush, it cared for them when they were sick and helped them when they were destitute and it shaped their religious ideology. Thanks to the church the people understood themselves as a holy remnant in North America, the seedbed of a Catholic civilization.

Industrialization began in Quebec at the turn of the twentieth century . While Quebec continued to see itself as a rural society defined by values appropriate for agricultural life, the industrialized sector grew rapidly. Generation of hydroelectric power and mining were the main industries, accompanied by manufacturing, especially of textiles and shoes. This was labour-intensive production for which Quebec offered a pool of cheap labour. The industries were owned by Anglo capital: British, Canadian and American. While many churchmen encouraged this industrialization as a source of work and income,[2] the church as a whole continued to speak of Quebec as an agricultural society and held up the rural life, especially clearing new land, as the ideal form of French-Canadian existence.

Yet Quebecers moved into cities in ever greater numbers. The church dealt with this population shift by creating a multitude of new parishes in the cities: thanks to the dedication of large numbers of priests and religious, the city population was able to be integrated into a stable and cohesive parish life as if they had never left the country. Urbanization did not weaken the value of kinship.[3] The great emphasis on large families in the country was continued in the city where it created grave economic problems. Thanks to the church's population policy French Canadians multiplied at a high rate and held their own against Anglo Canadians who greatly increased their numbers through immigration from Britain and later from continental European countries. French Canadians fought the conquest with *the revenge of the cradle.* Neither the break-up of cohesive communities nor the decline of religious devotion accompanied the first phase of industrial modernization.

What did not take place during this time was the political modernization of Quebec. By political modernization I mean the growing role of government in fostering and ordering the life of society.[4] Because Quebec's government resisted the efforts of the federal

government to expand its powers, the province retained jurisdiction over education, health care and matters of public welfare. Yet Quebec did not want direct
responsibility for these areas: it preferred to leave these
tasks to private organizations, especially the Catholic
church which in the past had exercised these functions.
The provincial government and the Catholic church
were content with the old order. The guardians of the
old order even resisted the welfare money occasionally
offered by the federal government to Quebec's poor.

Maurice Duplessis, premier of Quebec from the
mid-thirties to the end of the fifties and acknowledged
boss and master of Quebec society, developed a political philosophy of *anti-statism*. He permitted the Catholic church, which gave him considerable support, to
remain the province's ideological guide. Despite the
new conditions created by industrialization, he wanted
the church to continue its involvement in education,
health services and social welfare. Premier Duplessis
was a reactionary. While he claimed to be a nationalist,
he did not intervene to curb the exploitative practices of
foreign corporations and the humiliation of his own
people; in fact, he invited the corporations to come to
Quebec, recommending its cheap and pacified labour
force. Premier Duplessis opposed the formation of unions. He rejected government involvement in public
services, especially hydro-electric power. Because he
vehemently opposed social change, he became the defender of the predominant Catholic ideology and re-
pressed religious and secular minorities that threatened
to undermine its spiritual sway. The convergence of
these different trends gave the Catholic church a power
and a presence with few historical parallels in a largely
industrialized society.[5] With funds made available by
the government, the church was responsible for the
educational system from primary school to university,
for hospitals and other health services and for assist-
ance to the poor and destitute. Though church and state

were legally separate, in actual fact the church was deeply involved in promoting and ordering social life and exercised considerable influence on government decisions, not least by being the principal source of the public ideology. In the mid-twentieth century this was an astonishing situation.

The English-speaking minority in Quebec, which included the industrial, commercial and financial elite, looked upon the province as a remnant of the past — half sanctuary, half museum. Still, because of the provincial government's non-interference policy, English-speaking Quebecers were not unhappy. The power elite was able to retain and expand economic control over the province and could count on a well-behaved working class with modest material aspirations. Able to organize their own social institutions, schools, universities, hospitals and welfare agencies, English-speaking Quebecers did not even have to learn French. Instead they expected upwardly mobile French Quebecers to learn English. French-speaking Canadian workers would learn only enough English to understand the orders given by the factory foreman

With the fall of Premier Duplessis' party and the election of a Liberal government on June 22, 1960 all this changed. What took place was the rapid political modernization of Quebec society. The new government regarded itself as the principal agent responsible for promoting Quebec society. This had a dramatic effect on the educational system, health care and public welfare, and more especially on economic life. The new government tried to restrain the power of foreign corporations, promote industries owned and managed by French Canadians and strengthen the participation of French Canadians in industrial and commercial life. These changes were accompanied by an extraordinarily popular enthusiasm, a new pride in being French Canadian and an outburst of cultural creativity.

Great changes took place in education.[6] In the past the church had shown more interest in cultural and religious instruction than in preparing the people for participation and competition in a technological age. Quebecers felt that they were ill prepared for the needs of modern society. For the French-speaking Canadian elite — doctors, lawyers and owners of small manufacturing and commercial enterprises — the church had devised a classical education of high quality. This elite was to make Quebec society the bearer of a higher, more spiritual civilization than the business civilization characteristic of North America. The new government created a ministry of education, which in turn devised a totally new educational program. The new system aimed at creating a Quebec population well-trained in scientific and technological matters. The ministry secularized the universities and created new institutions of higher learning to prepare French Canadians to play a more active role in their own society. Eventually the government created ministries of health and public welfare.

As rapid secularization occurred, the Catholic church found itself excluded from functions it had exercised over the years. The old Catholic ideology was replaced by a new, secular philosophy of self-determination with a double focus: one on modernization and political participation to catch up with other industrial societies; the other on the preservation of national identity, the enhancement of Quebec culture and the creation of a new French presence in North America. The extraordinary cultural activity generated by the Quiet Revolution is a subject that outside Quebec has not attracted the attention it deserves.

Who was the agent of the Quiet Revolution? In whose interest did the government act? In a general sense, it is possible to say that the entire people strove for a position of equality in the Canadian confederation. Either equality or independence, the slogan ran. Was it correct to speak of Quebec as suffering oppression in Canada? This controversial question deserves a reply.

Were Quebecers an oppressed people?

Quebec is a province within confederation; it always has had its provincial government, working entirely in French and exercising responsibility for a wide area of social and cultural life. Quebec, like the other provinces, is represented in the federal parliament at Ottawa. In parliament English and French are the two official languages. French Canadians have often supplied prime ministers and members of Canada's federal cabinet. These institutional realities do not allow a comparison between French Canadians and other minority peoples such as Mexican Americans. The francophone culture of Quebec is protected by a multitude of institutions. At the same time, francophone culture has always been threatened because it has a minority status on the North American continent and because technology, science and business operated almost exclusively in English. A number of scholars argue that Quebec and some other provinces suffer from regional disparity and from exploitation by large foreign-owned corporations, but that it is misleading to speak of Quebec as an oppressed society. Because confederation did not produce the equalization of the provinces which it had promised, there are Canadian provinces worse off than Quebec. The counter argument, offering more convincing evidence, proposes that there exists in Quebec a combination of economic and national (linguistic, ethnic, cultural) patterns of subordination that makes Quebec's situation unique among the provinces and fully justifies the adjective "oppressed." (Still, this oppression cannot be compared with the massive subjugation inflicted on Canada's Native peoples.)

Every sociological study of Quebec's economic life has demonstrated the subordinate position of French Canadians. Everett Hughes' *French Canada in Transition,* published in the early forties, examined Quebec's small industrial towns.[7] The study presents a deeply divided society, with the English in the upper ranks of the industries and the French in the lower. The English occupied leadership positions on every level. Examination of the authority structure in non-industrial occupations confirms the same social hierarchy. Hughes shows that the society was organized in such a way that the English minority was not obliged to learn French: wherever the French and the English had occasion to meet, conversation was carried on in English. John Porter's *The Vertical Mosaic*, published twenty years later, comes to the identical conclusion in the section called "British and French: Higher and Lower Charter Groups."[8] In the late sixties the Royal Commission on Bilingualism and Biculturalism, relying on census data, showed that French Canadians were at a greater occupational disadvantage in 1961 than they had been in 1941.[9] Even after ten years of the Quiet Revolution, the 1971 census gave no evidence that the disadvantaged position of French Canadians was improving. This massive phenomenon is more than regional disparity; it represents the economic subordination of a people. The existence of a minority of French Canadians in high positions in industry, finance and commerce does not invalidate this conclusion. The pattern of upper and lower has been stable. The word "oppression" is justified here. Disadvantages imposed on Quebecers in the linguistic, cultural and political realms served to protect their economic subservience and to that extent may be called oppression.

The role of the church in this historical context is not without ambiguity. On one hand the creation of a powerful Catholic ideology helped the people to withstand assimilation and decline; it created for them an independent cultural identity that during the Quiet Revolution served as resource for the political struggle. At the same time, the same Catholic ideology prevented

Quebecers from keeping up with modern education and from competing successfully with English-speaking Canadians in their society. The same ideology, so much at odds with North American life, created in Quebecers a sense that they were different. While they acknowledged this difference with spiritual pride, they also knew the shadow of self-doubt. They sometimes felt like a people caught in the past, left behind by modern developments. In a certain sense, then, the whole people, in search of its own power and a new, more contemporary culture, was the carrier of the Quiet Revolution.

Who were the immediate carriers of the Quiet Revolution? Sociologists who have examined the question offer varying explanations,[10] It seems that several sectors of the middle classes had an urgent economic interest in the victory of the Liberal party and the modernization of society. First of all, the large administrative elite employed by the church to serve in education, health and social welfare already had become restless in the fifties. Mainly lay people, they yearned for greater independence from episcopal control, for improved efficiency and wider extension of public services and for access to the fiscal resources of the government. Some well-known priests, especially Gérard Dion and Louis O'Neil, also promoted Quebec's political modernization during the fifties.[11] Catholic political progressivism was supported by the Catholic Action movement, inspired by ideas prominent in Catholic social thought in France. In 1960 a Christian Brother anonymously produced *Les insolences du Frère Untel*, a controversial bestseller which expressed the yearning for a more liberal, more educated, more responsible and more modern society.[12]

Secondly, there was a sector of reasonably successful French-Canadian middle managers at large industrial and financial corporations whose promotions were barred by the unwritten rule that French Canadians could not move to the top. They favoured the new nationalism and a modernizing government that would make French the working language of Quebec and allow French Canadians to rise to the highest positions. Another sector of Quebec's traditional elite — the owners of small institutions of commerce, finance and light industry — felt great pressure from American and Anglo-Canadian corporations which tried to buy or squeeze them out of existence. These small businessmen were eager to have a provincial government that would protect French-Canadian economic and industrial institutions.

Finally, several sectors of society greatly desired the creation of a ministry of education that would introduce a more technologically-oriented educational curriculum. Among them were members of the middle and lower classes who blamed the subordination of French Canadians in industry and commerce partly on the unrealistic education provided by the church. To succeed Quebec needed a new system of schools and universities. The spread of industrial technology made even the English-speaking managers of large corporations eager to have their French-Canadian work force better educated and better prepared to acquire technical skills. These were the sectors behind the political movement that initiated and carried forward the Quiet Revolution.

Rapid secularization

Secularization was rapid. The church lost control over a wide range of social institutions, especially in education, health and welfare. It also lost control of the symbols by which Quebec society defined itself. The new secular nationalism, with a liberal and later with a socialist perspective, became the new public philosophy. The church also suffered an enormous loss in membership. It is curious how quickly vast numbers of Catholics, trained and often fervent in their disciplined religion, shed the faith of their ancestors. While

Catholicism remains visible in Quebec culture — in the historical memories, architecture, public symbols and the saints' names given to villages, towns and organizations — practising Catholics have become a minority.

In a widely-read 1982 article Raymond Lemieux, a sociologist at Laval University, writes that practising Catholics represent about forty percent of the population.[13] Studies of church attendance and sacramental participation show that religious practice is very uneven. The significant variable is here the stability of the community. Where stability has been preserved, especially in the country and small towns, religious practice is often as high as seventy percent; in the large cities, especially in areas where social mobility is high, religious participation is low. Yet even the cities show considerable variation. Wherever we find a stable community, religious practice is still up to fifteen percent, while in areas of largely transient population the practice is as low as seven percent. Under the influence of Vatican II, the late sixties spawned a very large number of base communities in the cities, especially in Montreal and Quebec, but the number of these groups has declined drastically since then.

How have the bishops reacted to the Quiet Revolution? They did not fight modernization, nor did they identify with the conservative sector of the population, as did the hierarchies in many Catholic countries. Instead, the bishops took time to reflect and in the spirit of Vatican ll sought a new definition of the church's mission in society. In 1968 they appointed a study commission — made up of pastors, theologians and social scientists and presided over by Fernand Dumont, a layperson and well-known Quebec sociologist — with the mandate to examine the church's identity crisis and make proposals for new pastoral directions. I know of no other national Catholic hierarchy that has commissioned an inquiry of this kind. By 1972, when the volumes of the Dumont Report were published, the original enthusiasm for renewal and creative experiment had greatly declined.[14] Still the Report had considerable impact. It recommended that the church recognize the inevitability of political modernization and cultural pluralism and resign itself to the loss of its institutional power and prestige. It asked the church to abandon the idea that Quebec was still a Catholic culture in which the Christian faith could, like the French language, simply be passed on from one generation to the next. The church should chart a new course, redefine its role in Quebec society and remain present — as one moral voice among several — to the collective project of building a modern, just and humane society. The Report argues that the bishops must rely on the help and co-operation of the entire Catholic community for this effort. Parishes have to become centres of discussion and dialogue where people express what Jesus Christ means to them today, what significance discipleship has for them and how they conceive of the place and function of the church in these times. The church is not simply a given; rather, it is a social and religious project which involves the entire believing community, with the bishops serving as leaders.

Like all reports of this kind the Dumont Report was implemented half-heartedly or not at all. Still it was influential. It affected the Catholic theology taught at seminaries and theological faculties in Quebec. In the dioceses where the Report was taken seriously, it created a new spiritual climate; and in dioceses where it was neglected, it generated discontent among progressive Catholics who saw more clearly what the church was and what it could be. To this day the Report remains an important ecclesiastical document.

David Martin's theory of modernization

As I studied the dynamic character of Quebec's shaken Catholicism, I sought a wider theoretical framework for the secularizing process in Quebec society. I was greatly impressed by David Martin's book, *A General Theory of Secularization*, which offers an invaluable comparative study of the various national Catholicisms in the modern period.[15] Martin, following the method of historical sociology, proposes and, I think, demonstrates that religion affects the way a traditional society moves into modernization. Martin wisely avoids causal language. He regards religion as a clue to a better understanding of the modernization process. His proposal is, therefore, open to theories that regard religion itself as strongly affected by infrastructural conditions. Martin demonstrates that the Protestant and Catholic forms of Christian faith have guided societies into modernity in significantly different ways. A comparative study of European and non-European Christian societies allows him to make several important generalizations. Wherever these generalizations have exceptions, Martin offers historical explanations for them. In this essay we shall pay attention only to one particular application of his general theory.

In general, Martin argues, the way Protestant societies moved into modernization produced pluralism, tolerance and democratic co-operation of different interest groups. Martin speaks here of a "cumulative legitimation"[16] of society: by this he means that different groupings of society, whether religious or secular, regional or economic, may be in conflict with one another, but have their own way of legitimating society as a whole. Protestantism has produced a cultural imagination that fosters pluralism; thus, the advance of secularization was not accompanied by great hostility to religion.

Over against this, Catholicism has produced an imagination that fosters totality. Catholicism has provided little room for dissent. Since Catholicism presented itself as the ideology of the whole, it was impossible to reject one aspect of the system and remain loyal to the rest. It was all or nothing. Those who dissented on one issue had to reject the system in its entirety and define themselves against inherited Catholicism. Because they rejected the whole the dissenters were in turn obliged to create their own totality. This imagination of totality guided Catholic societies into modernization. What happened in these countries was a tragic cultural schism.

As the modernizing sector of society defined itself against Catholicism, the church identified itself with the conservative forces resisting modernization. As a result the whole of society became divided into two camps with Catholics on one side and liberals on the other. Later it was Catholics on one side and socialists on the other. The Catholic tradition discouraged cumulative legitimation. On the contrary, it tended to universalize conflicts in society. In the Catholic countries the conflict among economic classes and different regions easily took on the character of a total struggle. Martin illustrates this interpretation with many historical examples. He demonstrates how useful this paradigm is in the study of the modernization process in the Catholic countries of Europe and Latin America.

There were exceptions to the rule. Some Catholic societies in Europe entered modernity without experiencing the cultural split between religion and irreligion. Martin pays detailed attention to modernization in the "mixed pattern" of such societies as Germany, Holland and Switzerland, where the Catholic minority represented about forty percent of the population and existed as heir of an age-old regional tradition. These are historical cases of special interest. Important in the context of this essay, however, are other exceptions to the Catholic pattern analysed by Martin. They are of two types. The first includes Ireland and Poland; the second, Belgium.[17]

Poland and Ireland were Catholic societies subjugated by empire. Several times the Polish people experienced division, with one sector assigned to Russian rule, one to Austrian and one to Prussian. Poland became an independent modernizing nation only after World War I. Similarly Ireland suffered British domination. It achieved independence during World War I. Under foreign rule and oppression the Catholic church became the symbol of resistance and identity. The people supported the church in their quest for collective survival. In this situation, Martin argues, the entry into modernization was not accompanied by a cultural split; on the contrary, the workers, the rising middle classes and the intellectuals remained loyal to the church. With the help of the peasants, craftsmen and small merchants (and in Poland the aristocracy) the church exercised enormous power and could suppress dissent in the sectors of the population affected by modernization. Still the workers, the middle class and the intellectuals allowed themselves to be dominated. To protect the unity and survival of their society they were willing to fit their social struggle into the overall Catholic framework.

Exemplifying the second type of exception was Belgium, a Catholic society which moved into modernization without a cultural schism. The reason for this, Martin argues, was that the creation of an independent Belgian state in the 1830s involved two movements: the liberal struggle against external control, mainly from France, and the Catholic struggle against domination by Protestant Holland. Because of this coincidence, the liberal constitution of Belgium guaranteed the rights and the freedom of the Catholic church. The tensions between Catholics and secular liberals (and secular socialists), while often bitter, never took on a radical form: each side of the conflict recognized that the other belonged to the very foundation of Belgian society.

Martin's theory, I suggest, sheds light on the modernization of Quebec society. Some may argue that Canada is really a "mixed society" with proportions of Protestants and Catholics similar to those in Germany,

Holland and Switzerland, and that Martin's analysis of mixed societies is appropriate for understanding Canadian society. Instead I argue that French Canadians understand themselves as a people, and Quebec society regards itself as the social, cultural and political embodiment of this people, even if important minorities of French Canadians live in other provinces and a substantial minority of English-speakers lives in Quebec. In the mixed societies of Germany, Holland and Switzerland the Catholic part of the population does not regard itself as a people.

My thesis is the following: I contend that Quebec society has moved into modernization without producing the cultural schism that has characterized Catholic societies. To understand what happened in the first phase of modernization (which we called industrial modernization), from 1900 to the end of the 1950s, the Polish-Irish exception is a useful paradigm; to understand what happened during the political modernization of the Quiet Revolution, the Belgian exception offers a helpful hint.

In the first period of industrialization the loyalty to the church of workers, rising middle class and intellectuals can be explained in terms of the Quebec experience of national oppression. In the second period, beginning in 1960, the absence of a cultural schism despite widespread secularization can be explained by the union of two movements, active at the beginning of the Quiet Revolution: the secular trend toward modernization and the religious renewal sparked by Vatican Council II.

Modernization before 1960

During the period from the turn of the century to the end of the fifties, Quebec remained thoroughly Catholic. This has been amply documented by historians.[18] The workers, the middle classes and the intellectuals remained loyal to the church's tradition. I have called this the Polish-Irish exception. Let me recall some of the historical evidence for this loyalty.[19]

From the beginning of industrialization the ecclesiastical leadership was greatly worried about the future of the labour movement.[20] In 1911 we see the foundation of the "École sociale populaire," an adult education centre to promote the church's teaching on labour. Early in the century, French-Canadian workers were organized under the auspices of the American Federation of Labor in its Canadian section, the Trades and Labour Congress. Yet the ecclesiastics were dissatisfied. They envisaged the creation of Catholic trade unions, where the workers would receive religious instruction, be taught the church's social doctrine, be protected against radicalism and be assured of their French-Canadian identity. In 1921 Catholic labour unions were founded. Their chaplains, appointed by the bishops, were responsible for the education of the workers, but they also had authority to influence the unions' decisions. Through the chaplains the bishops were able to guide and direct the working class. Compared to the labour struggles in English Canada the union movement in Quebec was tame. This was true even during the depression of the thirties. The bishops remained in charge. When in the late forties the labour movement became more combative — the asbestos strike of 1949 was a warning to the establishment — the striking workers had the support of a significant sector of the church: a few bishops, some priests, the Catholic Action movement and a large number of non-organized, liberal-minded Catholic lay people.[21] Under these conditions even the more aggressive unions felt no need to distance themselves from Catholicism.

What ideas defined the social aspirations of Quebec's middle class in this period? I will mention two of them: corporatism and nationalism. Neither, it must be said, promoted a realistic political movement to transform

Quebec society.[22] Studies of these ideologies produced by contemporary Quebec scholars have drawn attention to their apolitical character. They offered only abstract, cultural ideals and utterly failed to generate concrete policies that could become the platform for a political movement. There is one exception to this rule I shall mention below. Corporatism, a social theory drawn from the church's official teaching, especially Pius XI's *Quadragesimo anno*, envisaged society as a social body kept alive and well through the co-operation of the various industries, trades and professions.[23] The participation of people in the decisions affecting their lives was to occur through corporations representing their productive activities: the industries, trades and professions. Corporatism was silent about political parties and parliamentary democracy. Corporatism envisaged a society in which all sectors, owners of industry as well as workers, accepted common norms of justice and a common social faith. The owning classes would then serve the well-being of the workers, and the workers, satisfied with just wages, would labour for the advancement of the common good. In a Catholic society such as Quebec, the promotion of corporatism involved first of all a call for spiritual renewal, an effort to strengthen the common faith. Since this theory had no relation to the existing political system in Canada and Quebec, it remained abstract and powerless.

Some Catholics committed to the corporatist vision of social justice looked with a certain longing to countries like Portugal where seemingly good Catholic leaders, unencumbered by parliamentary democracy, translated Catholic ideals into political reality. To some Quebecers, even Mussolini appeared for a time like a good Catholic leader.

The nationalism of this period was also largely of clerical origin.[24] After the defeat of the secular, forward-looking nationalism of *les patriotes* of 1837 — rebels inspired by the ideas of the French Revolution — the

Catholic bishops were able to link nationalist sentiment to the propagation of the Catholic faith. Fidelity to Catholicism, they believed, would enable French Canadians to survive on a hostile continent and create their own collective identity. After the industrialization beginning in 1900, many clerics, the best known of whom was Lionel Groulx, wanted to protect French-Canadian identity against the onslaught of Protestantism, secularism, materialism and English-speaking modernity by fostering an intense nationalism based on past glories, a romanticized vision of French-Canadian religious history. *Les Canadiens* were a chosen people, a faithful remnant, the bearers of a Catholic civilization in Protestant/secular North America. They were now to close ranks, resist modern liberal ideas, preserve their language and faith and struggle for greater independence from English Canada and its central agent, the federal government, even at the price of relative poverty and backwardness according to the norms of English Canada. This backward-looking nationalism — clerical in origin, sometimes accompanied by xenophobia, anti-semitism and yearnings for a strong leader who would lift society out of the morass of democracy — was endorsed by wide sectors of the middle class and intellectuals.

In the thirties, in the depths of the depression, the only political movement that could be called radical was Action libérale nationale (A.L.N.), a movement that turned nationalist sentiment against foreign ownership of the industries and advocated their take-over by the provincial government.[25] The A.L.N. recommended the taming of capitalism by government and the promotion of small industries owned by French Canadians; it favoured unionization, a new labour code protecting workers from exploitation, and government-sponsored insurance for workers and farmers, covering unemployment, sickness and old age pensions. In the Quebec context this was a radical program. At the same time, the A.L.N. stood entirely within Catholicism. The first draft of its platform had in fact been written by a group of clerics. The movement sought the support of the people by showing that its radical economic program was backed by elements of Catholic social teaching. Despite initial success, the A.L.N. did not last long. It was co-opted by Maurice Duplessis, and made part of a new political party, the Union nationale, which quickly lost interest in social and economic reform.

In the fifties when massive post-war industrialization created new social conditions, the regime of Maurice Duplessis seemed wholly out of touch with the social reality of Quebec. There was growing unrest among the workers and among members of the middle class, especially the intellectuals who stood for modernization, scientific education, political democracy, individual responsibility and imaginative enterprise. A new review, *Cité libre*, founded in 1951 became the organ for the promotion of liberal ideas.[26] In its pages young intellectuals, many later prominent in the new Quebec or in the federal government, demanded the modernization of Quebec. Pierre Trudeau, later prime minister of Canada, was a frequent contributor. *Cité Libre* believed that it was time Quebec caught up with modern, North American society. What was necessary were the overhauling of the educational system and the acceptance of liberal ideals: civil liberties, pluralism of opinions, the strengthening of democracy, and popular participation. Though hostile to the reigning order in Quebec, *Cite Libre* remained wholly within the spiritual world of Catholicism. It looked toward progressive Catholic intellectuals writing in France, among whom was the famous Emmanuel Mounier, founder and editor of the review *Esprit*, who advocated a new, more positive Catholic approach to modernity. *Esprit* warned Catholics against the traditional identification with the conservative forces in society; because of its sympathy with socialism *Esprit* defended the right of government to protect the common good, interfere with the free market and assure a greater share for the poor in the wealth of society. Whatever the religious convictions of the contributors to *Cité Libre* were, they certainly presented themselves as proponents of a modernizing and secularizing movement solidly rooted in Catholic faith.

During this first phase of industrialization Quebec remained Catholic. Because of Quebec's peculiar position, the workers, the middle class and the intellectuals remained loyal to Catholicism. Some may argue that the Catholic church was powerful enough to force these social sectors of society to toe the line. Still, these groups were willing to be thus forced. The church still symbolized for them their collective identity and their refusal to assimilate to Anglo North American culture.

Modernization after 1960

The Quiet Revolution produced an explosion in Quebec society leading to rapid secularization. The church lost its institutional power in the field of education, health care and public welfare; it ceased to be the symbol-maker of society; and, in a single decade, it lost at least fifty percent of its members.[27] Yet this entry into political modernization was not accompanied by cultural schism. Catholic and secular forces did not line up in mutual hostility and divide the population as has happened in so many Catholic societies. Why not? Because as with the Belgian exception the political thrust toward modernization in the early sixties was based on the union of two distinct movements — the secular, political movement for a new, self-reliant, democratic Quebec and the Catholic renewal movement sparked by Vatican Council II.

What I will have to show in this final section of my essay is first of all that there was affinity and co-operation between secular reform and Catholic renewal at the beginning of the Quiet Revolution and, secondly, that

Quebec society has not suffered a cultural schism despite the massive secularization in the subsequent decade. What has come to characterize Quebec society is compromise between secular and Catholic forces; what has come to characterize the Quebec Catholic church is its ready acknowledgment of pluralism within its own ranks.

The collective excitement in Quebec after the victory of the Liberal Party on June 22, 1960 assumed extraordinary proportions. The people, especially the youth, rapidly demanded participation in building a modern Quebec. They were ready for political organization and collective action. A cultural outburst took place, especially in Montreal and Quebec City. An unexpected creativity emerged in music, poetry, song, drama and all the arts. Intellectual activity entered a heightened phase. Catholics participated in this excitement. The Quiet Revolution repudiated the old Quebec, the Catholic Quebec; it dreamt of a new, modern Quebec — a free, pluralistic society, yet faithful to itself, its language, its roots and its people. Thanks to the ferment created by Vatican ll, Catholics were able to contrast the old, authoritarian church with the new, conciliar church; the static Catholicism of the past with the dynamic Catholicism of the present. The harsh language of repudiation that usually accompanies a secular, liberal, modernizing movement in a Catholic society did not shock these Catholics because they, too, repudiated the church of the past. New Catholic guidelines, formulated as the Vatican Council held its sessions, allowed Catholics to participate in the secularization movement of the Quiet Revolution. They welcomed the removal of the church from its monopolistic involvement in education, health and welfare; they recognized the appropriateness of the church's loss of its ideological monopoly; and they approved of the new social pluralism.

Documentation for this religious phenomenon is not difficult to find. The Dominican Order, strongly influenced by progressive theologians, exercised a wide pastoral ministry favourable to the new Quebec. Their review, *La revue dominicaine*, was replaced by the new *Maintenant*, a monthly addressed to a wide readership, dedicated to what was then called "dialogue between church and world." *Maintenant* favoured pluralism; it did not lament the curbing of ecclesiastical power; it approved of the challenge to the Catholic monopoly; it gave expression to what it regarded as the new Catholicism defined by Vatican II. While it did not abandon a critical stance toward the new political developments, it fully shared in the excitement of Quebecers over the Quiet Revolution. The daring approach of *Maintenant* is particularly apparent in comparison with the review, *Relations*, published by the Jesuits, which at that time remained wedded to the old Quebec and the old church. Eventually *Maintenant* editor Vincent Harvey, OP, got into trouble with the ecclesiastical authorities and was removed from his post because he was allegedly ahead of his time. Under a new editor *Maintenant* carried forward the same message. Many authors associated with *Maintenant* became active in the Liberal Party and later joined the Parti Québécois (PQ). A few years later some of the authors were active in the ministries of the newly elected PQ provincial government.

Les insolences du Frère Untel, [28] the best-seller already mentioned, produced a furor in a society where self-criticism had been unwelcome. Brother Anonymous, later recognized as Pierre-Jérôme Desbiens, criticized the old church in the name of the new. He offered a scathing portrait of Quebec society — its corruption in politics, the weakness of its educational system, the irrelevance of the church in the modern age and the decline of the French spoken in Quebec. The author was sent out of the country; he too was regarded as ahead of his time. Yet his critical reflections released cultural and religious forces that joined the Quiet Revolution and the building of the new Quebec. We see in this little book the emergence of a new national pride wholly at odds with the backward-looking, clerical nationalism of the twenties and thirties: a pride in Quebec as a nation struggling to become a free society. The new, democratic nationalism had affinities with that of the 1837 rebels, who were inspired by the ideals of the French Revolution.

A visible symbol of the conflict between the old and the new in the Quebec church was the imposing figure of Cardinal Paul-Émile Léger, Archbishop of Montreal. At one time the archbishop had been a man of the old school: he stood for a powerful church in a Quebec faithful to the old values. The story is told that when he returned from Rome in 1953 after having received the red hat of the cardinalate, Léger called out to the Montreal crowd waiting for him at the airport, freely improvising on a psalm, "You have made yourself beautiful, O Montreal, to receive your prince." Years later, during the preparations for the Vatican Council, Cardinal Léger turned away from the triumphalism of the past and recognized that the church must seek a new place in a pluralist society. He stood for the critical adaptation of Catholicism to the needs of contemporary men and women and came to believe that "service" was the word best able to express the church's mission in the modern world. At the Vatican Council, Léger became a powerful spokesman for the new Catholicism, even though this cost him the friendship of members of the Roman Curia and of several Quebec bishops. In the historical context of Quebec society, a change of direction in ecclesiastical matters symbolized support for the Quiet Revolution and the new Quebec.

Compromise and pluralism

My second point pertains to the search for a compromise between secular and religious forces. Among the first actions of the Liberal government in 1960 was the decision to reform the entire educational system.

The aim was to take education out of the hands of the church and create a ministry of education responsible for an education that would meet the needs of a modern society. Preparation of the reform bill and the creation of the education ministry took several years. Before the government submitted the reform bill to the national assembly in 1964, it had engaged in confidential dialogue with the bishops and after some bargaining obtained their approval. The bishops had decided not to oppose the law that would exclude them from their position of power and responsibility in the field of education. In return the government made an offer to them: the new bill would leave untouched the confessional character of the Quebec school system.[29] Primary and secondary education was divided into separate Catholic and Protestant schools. The French schools of the majority were almost without exception Catholic. English schools were on the whole Protestant. The English-speaking Catholic minority had its own Catholic schools. Atheists, Jews, Muslims and members of other religions had to send their children to the English-speaking Protestant schools. The government in the sixties was willing to tolerate these irrationalities and to leave the confessional character of the schools untouched. The new bill took from the Catholic church the legal responsibility for the Catholic school system. The ministry assumed this task while the church retained the right to appoint chaplains to these schools to act as liturgists, counsellors and, if need be, as religion teachers. The ministry of education, moreover, was to be assisted by an educational council, which included representatives of the Catholic bishops. The compromise seemed satisfactory to both government and church hierarchy.

Despite the extraordinary power which the Catholic church exercised over the institutions and the consciences of French Canadians, the rapid secularization of the Quiet Revolution produced no political

anticlericalism. There were and still are many Quebecers who are angry with the church and repudiated it as an obstacle to personal freedom and collective creativity. There has been anticlerical sentiment in Quebec literature and among artists since the thirties. To this day many stage plays, performed before applauding audiences, express resentment against the domination formerly exercised by the church. But anticlericalism has never become public policy. No party or candidate seeking election for public office, low or high, would ever make an anti-ecclesiastical remark in the hope of gaining wider support. Although their journals have occasionally published anticlerical articles, left-wing intellectuals have not directed their public criticism against the inherited religion. There are practising Catholics in their ranks, and they do not wish to repudiate these comrades.

The historical record shows that the rapid entry into secularization was characterized not by a secular-Catholic cultural schism but by compromise and pluralism. The compromise was sought by the Catholic bishops when they gave their approval to the educational reform in the early sixties, when they appointed the Dumont Commission to examine the crisis of the church, and when, more recently, they adopted a flexible position in response to various efforts by the government to rationalize the Quebec school system.

The division of public education into a Catholic and Protestant system has become increasingly anachronistic. On the one hand, the number of French-Canadian parents who do not want a Catholic education for their children is constantly growing. At present these parents must send their children to a Catholic school. Children have the right to opt out of religious instruction, but many Quebecers consider doing so a burden on the children. Why should children be made to feel that they must choose against an established order? Secondly, since the legislation introduced by the Parti Québécois

demands that immigrants and people from outside the province send their children to the French school system, it seems increasingly inappropriate to offer them only Catholic schools. Perhaps the supreme contradiction is that non-Catholic children who have the right to be educated in English must be educated in the Protestant school system, whatever their religion or lack thereof.

These and other reasons prompted the Parti Québécois government to announce a second reform of public education. Catholic schools may have to go. Again, the bishops' reaction has been moderate. In the public debate, which deeply involved all sectors of society, Catholic leaders and Catholic groups adopted a variety of positions. There was no single Catholic stance over against a clearly defined secular position.

There is no room in this essay to give a complete analysis of the public debate on the Quebec school system during the late seventies.[30] Still, a summary may illustrate what I mean by compromise and pluralism. The terms of the debate were not secular schools versus Catholic schools. Instead Quebecers were discussing several possibilities. Some defended the Catholic school of the present, no longer under the authority of the church. Others proposed a pluralistic school, not aligned with Catholicism, but in principle open to religion as a cultural value and ready to supply religious instruction to the children who want it or whose parents desire it: such instruction would be Catholic, Protestant, Jewish or whatever. Finally there was talk of a secular "neutral" school, which would be removed from religion altogether. The government favoured the pluralistic school. This would allow those parts of Quebec that remained completely Catholic to have schools that reflected the common faith; at the same time schools in large cities characterized by pluralism would be able to adapt the education of children to the wishes of the parents and the community. Such a system would make

no one a second-class citizen. An equivalent English school system would also answer the pluralistic needs of the English-speaking community. What the present Catholic school would lose was a certain presence of the church in the person of the chaplain and in the form of the Catholic liturgy held on special school occasions. Still, pluralistic schools would not exclude the Catholic religion from the educational process.

The Quebec bishops were not totally united in response to these plans. Although they produced a joint statement, several bishops publicly expressed slightly deviating positions. In their joint declaration the bishops expressed regret about the disappearance of the Catholic school system. At the same time they recognized the rational need for changing the present arrangement. They had no objection to the introduction of pluralistic schools if this took place slowly, beginning with those parts of the province where the pluralism of the population demanded it, while leaving untouched for the time being the towns and villages where this pluralism was not yet present.

The then Archbishop of Montreal, Paul Grégoire, took a more conservative position. He asked the faithful of his diocese to struggle for the retention of the Catholic school system. Other bishops publicly adopted a position that was slightly more liberal than the joint declaration. These bishops gave a warmer welcome to the pluralistic school as a system of education that would allow the local community, pluralistic as it has become in many areas, to participate in the direction of its schools. This diversity in views is an interesting case of pluralism in the episcopate.

Catholic organizations offered a wide spectrum of opinions on the school question. A conservative organization, Les parents catholiques, asked for more than did Archbishop Grégoire. Dissatisfied with the present Catholic schools, these parents wanted them directly supervised by the Catholic hierarchy who were to

administer orthodoxy tests for all teachers of religion. Other Catholic organizations recommended different versions of the pluralistic school. There were even Catholic groups that supported neutral schools where religious instruction was to be replaced by moral education that would be beneficial for the whole society.

Despite wide support for transformation of the confessional school system, the P.Q. government was unable to change the inherited pattern. A court ruled that the existence of confessional schools was guaranteed by the British North America Act of 1867 for the cities of Montreal and Quebec (in those days, to protect the Protestant minority) and that therefore the proposed bill transforming confessional schools was unconstitutional. Still, the irrationality of Quebec's confessional school system is widely acknowledged. The succeeding Liberal government is again preparing a new bill, somewhat differently conceived, to deconfessionalize the schools. The government is receiving legal advice so that this time the courts are unlikely to sustain objections raised against it.

The school debate in Quebec society is an excellent illustration of my point in this section of the essay: that entry into secularization has not produced cultural schism but compromise and pluralism. What is peculiar about Quebec (and largely absent in English Canada and the United States) is that Catholic issues are part of the public debate involving the whole of society. The various positions Catholics adopt, be they bishops or lay people, are recorded and critically analysed in the daily press. Intra-Catholic debates have a cultural meaning that concerns all Quebecers, even if they have become quite secular.

I will give two more examples to show that in Quebec the response to public issues does not line up Catholics in a single front. The first is taken from the beginning of the Quiet Revolution. Sensing the need for modern, post-secondary education to prepare

Quebecers for competition with English-speaking Canadians, the Jesuits proposed to the government transforming their Collège Sainte-Marie into a new, up-to-date university. The proposal was vehemently opposed by many Quebecers.[31] They admitted that a new university was badly needed but objected to organizing it under the auspices of a religious order. They called for secular education by educators in touch with modern society and open to the aspirations of the new Quebec. This vehement public debate did not line up secularizers against Catholics. Many intellectuals who considered themselves faithful Catholics strongly opposed the Jesuit proposal. The professors of the University of Montreal, then still a Catholic university, organized a campaign against the creation of another Catholic university. The Jesuits who defended their project at first labelled their opponents as anticlerical and secular. This would have been a realistic judgment in a previous period of Quebec history. Yet the Jesuits soon realized that opposition to the project also came from committed Catholics, including the clergy. When the new university was founded several years later, it emerged out of antecedent educational structures of Collège Sainte-Marie but was completely and unambiguously secular.

The second example is taken from 1975 when Quebec's major labour organizations formed a Common Front to resist the government's effort to control them. The Common Front was able to organize a strike, sustained over many weeks, that affected the whole society by closing facilities such as schools and hospitals. The issue raised serious moral problems. As is customary in Quebec, even in the secular Quebec of the Quiet Revolution, Catholic bishops, Catholic organizations, and Catholic individuals expressed themselves in public on the moral issues of the day.[32] First of all a group of Catholics representing the social justice commissions of several dioceses published a joint statement. They affirmed the social project for a new Quebec initiated by the Quiet Revolution and argued that this project was now being undermined by the action of the Common Front. Too many people were made to suffer, especially the weak and the old, the very people that needed society's protection. The joint statement did not support the position of government and management; it only argued against the position taken by the Common Front. A little while later, a well-known Catholic priest and social scientist, Gérard Dion, gave a public address severely criticizing the Common Front. On the other hand, Bishop Adolphe Proulx of Hull made a public statement defending the workers and siding with the unions in their struggle for greater justice. The government seems so strong when dealing with workers, Bishop Proulx said, but it seems so weak when dealing with multinational corporations. A left-wing association of Catholic workers, Le mouvement des travailleurs chrétiens, published a statement fully supporting the Common Front. Finally, the Social Affairs Commission of the Quebec hierarchy brought out a pastoral letter dealing with the strike. In it the bishops, refusing to take sides in this labour dispute, vehemently urged greater responsibility on both sides because the number of people suffering from lack of services was constantly growing.

Examples of such debates could be multiplied. Catholics, though no longer a majority, are an identifiable presence in public life. As one historical source of Quebec life the church, though stripped of its former power, is expected to contribute to the public debate. A certain cultural confidence gives Catholic groups a strong sense that it is their responsibility to participate in public discussions and they do not hesitate to reveal to the public the disagreements within the Catholic community. Catholicism in Quebec has become pluralistic.

Committed and vocal Catholics are found in all political parties and social organizations. This is true of the traditional parties including the Parti Québécois. In the seventies the cabinet of Premier René Lévesque included two ecclesiastics, Louis O'Neil, a well-known priest-scholar who had resigned from the priesthood, and Jacques Couture, a former Jesuit who had become a secular priest to get permission to enter political life. Even in the labour unions and socialist organizations Catholics were strongly represented.

In the seventies Catholic pastoral organizations with a left-wing political perspective exercised their ministry among the working class and lower income people, *les classes populaires.* During those years, there was also a strong Catholic presence in the political organizations of the left. For this reason socialists, including those influenced by Marxism, did not define themselves in opposition to the Catholic religion. This was also true of two socialist movements formed in the early eighties. The 1981 manifesto, *Pour un Québec socialiste,* produced by the Committee of a Hundred, proposed a democratic socialism committed to equality between men and women, ecological concern and Quebec independence. The manifesto revealed a profound awareness of the cultural dynamics operative in the passage toward socialism; it contained not a single antireligious statement. The second 1981 movement, Le regroupement pour le socialisme, was oriented more toward local grassroots organization of workers and low income people. Though it betrayed no hint of hostility toward religion, it operated out of a more clearly defined neo-Marxist perspective. Committed Catholics were active in both movements, some specifically out of fidelity to their Christian faith.

No public debate in Quebec has ever created a neat division between believers and non-believers, not even the outrageous play, *Les fées ont soif,* which denounced devotion to Mary, widely practised in the old Quebec, as an ideology of women's enslavement! While the play appeared blasphemous to many Catholics and was condemned by Archbishop Grégoire of Montreal, it did not cause a cultural schism: Catholic feminist organizations and some active church people defended the aim and meaning of the play, even if they thought it was in bad taste.[33]

My conclusion is that the rapid secularization of this Catholic society has been characterized not by cultural schism but by compromise and pluralism. The reason for this remarkable development was that in the early sixties the affinity between two movements, one secular and one religious, allowed Catholic men and women faithful to their heritage to join the Quiet Revolution and to co-operate with their fellow citizens in the creation of a new society.

* * *

Catholics in Quebec have become a minority. Because young people are largely absent the future of the church is by no means assured. Still, the Catholic community includes many vital and imaginative elements, the Quebec conference of bishops not the least of them.

Chapter Two

The Dumont Report: Democratizing the Catholic Church

In the nineteenth century the Catholic church repudiated the emerging liberal society and the democratization of culture. For the church the authority to rule was derived from God, not from the people. In its own organization the church decided to swim against contemporary currents. By defining the pope's supreme jurisdiction Vatican Council I (1870) limited the decision-making power of the local authorities, the bishops, who became more or less administrative agents of the central authority, the papacy. The church was pleased to present itself to the world as an ecclesiastical monarchy, a pyramid of power, the antidemocratic symbol par excellence.

To what extent can large religious organizations resist the political ethos of their home societies? In the second half of the twentieth century, Catholics living in democratic cultures have found it increasingly difficult to accept the non-participatory, top-down exercise of authority practised in their own church. Dissatisfaction was widespread. In 1960 when Pope John XXIII convoked the second Vatican Council, the desire for more participatory structures and for the freedom to dissent was expressed in many quarters of the church.

Vatican Council II (1962-1965) made a modest contribution to democratizing the church. While it did not change the structure of the ecclesiastical organization, it did provide a doctrinal basis for the effort to make the life of the church more free and participatory.

First, Vatican II acknowledged that the Christian people participate in Christ's prophetic mission[1] and are teachers in the church. Since the Holy Spirit guides the church not simply through the hierarchy of popes and bishops but also through the gifts or charisms of the laity, the hierachy must be open to dialogue and listen to the Spirit speaking in the people.

Secondly, Vatican II made collegiality a mark of Catholic identity.[2] Strictly speaking, collegiality means that in the exercise of his supreme authority the Pope is not alone: he is surrounded by the college of bishops who collectively share this supreme authority. During a church council such as Vatican II this sharing takes place in a juridically defined institution; at other times, this sharing is not legally defined but depends on the initiative of the pope.

In a wider sense, collegiality refers to the exercise of authority on any level in the church. Collegiality demands that bishops be in dialogue with one another, with their priests and their people, and that in their domain priests be open to dialogue with the members of their parish.

These are just promises. Vatican II did not legislate any structural changes. Still, promises are important. In this case they undermine the theological foundation of the monarchical, pyramidal, antidemocratic church; they promote an alternative institutional ideal within the inherited papal-episcopal structure; they produce restlessness and irritation among Catholics faced with the Vatican's contemporary effort to restore the papal monarchy.

Can the Catholic church be democratized? Since Vatican II there have been several significant authoritative declarations and a few pratical experiments to widen participation in the church's life. Let me mention Pope John Paul II's surprising social teaching — new in the Catholic church — that people are meant to be the subjects or responsible agents of their society and of all the institutions to which they belong. John Paul II sees participation as a human right. He has written that governments confining decision-making to an elite group of whatever kind sin against the subjectivity of the people, rob people of their due, frustrate them and provoke them either to emigrate or to seek refuge in pure interiority.[3]

What does this mean? If democracy is defined — as it is in the liberal tradition — as a form of government that maximizes personal freedom, then it is irreconcilable with Roman Catholicism; but if democracy is defined as a form of goverment that maximizes participation, then it is acceptable to Roman Catholicism and not at odds with the institution of the church. This is the social teaching formulated by John Paul II, even though he has never applied it to the organization of the church.

According to a few, more daring ecclesiastical texts it is the church's mission to promote co-operation and participation in secular society; to do this the church itself must become a model of communion and participation.[4] These texts recognize that the church is a cultural agent and that its self-organization is not simply its own affair. For the style of its self-organization, whether elitist or participatory, influences society and encourages either an authoritarian or a democratic culture.

The most important practical experiment to introduce democracy into ecclesiastical life was that of the

Brazilian church. Here the church sought to re-organize itself through the creation of thousands of base communities, the massive participation of lay people in the church's pastoral mission, and the collegial, dialogue-promoting structure used by the bishops to exercise their authority. Much has been written about this development.[5] The new church model was approved by the 1979 Latin American Bishops Conference at Puebla, Mexico. Here communion and participation were urged as the ideal for the entire Latin American church.[6] Yet more recently, the Vatican has decided to discredit the Brazilian model and dismantle the participatory institutions set up in the progressive dioceses.[7]

The purpose and method of the Dumont Commission

In this chapter I will examine a remarkable ecclesiastical effort to introduce democracy into the church of Quebec. As is well-known, the Quiet Revolution of the sixties produced a rapid secularization of Quebec society. In those years, the people of Quebec sought a new collective self-definition not dependent on their Catholic past. The Quebec government took over the network of ecclesiastical organizations that had served society's welfare, health and education. This process was accompanied by a drastic drop in church membership.[8]

In 1968, the Quebec bishops appointed a research commission, with Fernand Dumont as president, to examine the contemporary crisis and to develop recommendations for new and more appropriate pastoral policies. In its structure, method and aim, the Dumont Commission resembled the study commissions set up by the federal and provincial governments, such as Quebec's famous 1966 Parent Commission which was established to examine the problems of the educational system in a society experiencing a rapid process of modernization and social change.

The Dumont Commission held hearings in various parts of Quebec and received briefs from church groups; it commissioned psycho-sociological research on the attitudes and religious values of the Quebec population; finally, it produced a report that analysed the present situation and made proposals for new pastoral policies. In 1971 the Commission published the report, *L'Église du Québec: un héritage, un projet*,[9] accompanied by two other volumes, one offering a new reading of the history of the Quebec church (1608-1970) and the other making available the psycho-sociological research to the public.[10] In 1972 the Commission published three more volumes: a history of Catholic Action in French Canada, a collection of the opinions and proposals gathered by the Commission, and a report synthesis for use in discussion groups.[11] Who were the members of the commission? The chairperson, Fernand Dumont, well-known sociologist, worked with eleven others including one bishop, a few priests and several laymen and women, drawn mainly from the Catholic Action movement. One member was identified with the trade unions.

The work of the Dumont Commission is very interesting from several points of view. My modest task in this chapter is to study the Dumont Report as an ecclesiastical effort to introduce democracy into the Quebec church.

To understand the work of the Dumont Commission it is necessary to look at the methodology used and explained at length in its report. The commission collected briefs from Catholic organizations, held hearings throughout the province and perused social scientific studies of the population's values and attitudes. How could the commission proceed from this empirical investigation to drafting its report, which had to take into account an enormous diversity of opinion? Extremely conservative Catholics wanted the church to return to the pre-conciliar, uniform style in teaching and liturgy.

Some of them even hoped that Quebec would again become a Catholic society. At the opposite end of the spectrum were radical Catholics who wanted the church to become fully egalitarian and this-worldly, to abandon the distinction between priesthood and laity and to involve itself in a mission defined in purely humanistic terms. Between these two extremes was a multitude of opinions and proposals.

Methodology is a problem for all commissions of this kind. Sometimes a commission is assigned a particular orientation. In that case the commission has certain principles that allow it to find its way through the briefs and opinions it has received. At other times the commission's mandate does not include a clear direction. In that case the members evaluate and discuss the materials submitted to them, hoping that this process will generate a consensus regarding the orientation to be pursued. This is what happened in the Parent Commission.[12] Eventually all its members agreed that, however great the merits of the existing educational system, the political, industrial and social changes in Quebec society were so drastic that a new educational system to prepare young people for the new society was required.

The Dumont Commission was allowed to define its own orientation. Following the Parent Commission it made the historical judgment that the Quiet Revolution was an irreversible process, that Quebec had become a secular, pluralistic society and that the Catholic church no longer spoke for the whole of Quebec but only for one sector, the community of the faithful. This judgment allowed the commission to disregard the submissions made by Catholics who yearned for the return of the old Quebec.[13]

The formulation of the second principle was much more difficult. The commission attached great importance to the concept of identity and argued that Quebec society and the Quebec church were both engaged in a quest to redefine their social identity.[14] The material submitted to the commission revealed Catholics' uncertainty in their search for collective existence. Thus the commission accepted the task of defining, or helping define, the identity of the Quebec church. In doing this the members were not neutral observers, relying simply on the judgment of engaged Catholics; the members saw themselves as believers struggling within the church and relying on its spiritual gifts to develop the church's collective identity in the new situation created by the Quiet Revolution. Phenomenological reflection on the development of personal and social identity convinced the commissioners that an identity crisis always demands both an original response to the new and the preservation of continuity. Both rupture and fidelity are needed. This twofold reference to past and future was the principle — this time a theological one — that guided the commission in its recommendations.[15] The commission decided to name this principle in its title for the final report, *L'Église du Québec: un héritage, un projet.*

The concept of "project" is new and daring in Catholic ecclesiology. The word recalls both Jean-Paul Sartre's understanding of the human being as *projet* and the public debate during the Quiet Revolution on Quebec society as a social project. Calling the church a project implies that it is not a static social reality, defined once and for all, but that, on the contrary, it is constantly being built by the Catholic community in the changing conditions of its history. What guides clergy and laity in this quest is a vision inspired by the Gospel and a critical analysis of the present situation. Responding to the vision and the analysis, the faithful choose a set of concrete objectives and aim at the creation of appropriate institutions to realize these objectives in the community.

This is precisely what the commission did in its report. It presented a vision shaped by scripture and the teaching of Vatican II; it analysed the crisis situation of the Quebec church; it outlined a set of objectives that to a certain degree incarnates the vision and recommended a modification of ecclesiastical institutions. In the report's words, pastoral policies are always *des stratégies du provisoire.* [16] The report pictured the church as forever unfinished, a people on pilgrimage or a series of workshops — *des chantiers* — where Catholics are jointly engaged in responding to the Gospel in the conditions of their day.

This ecclesial project is at the same time in continuity with the past. The church to be built is faithful to its inheritance. So serious was the commission's concern for the church's heritage that it demanded the writing of a special report later published under the title *Histoire de l'Église catholique au Québec, 1608-1970* that was to clarify the impact of Quebec society on the Quebec church during various periods. This report demonstrated that Quebec's political dependence as French colony, a British colony and later a Canadian province allowed the church to play a more important social role than is usually assumed by ecclesiastical institutions. The political situation of dependence also prompted the church to turn increasingly to Rome as source of its own power and independence. Both the *grandeur* and the *misère* of the Quebec church reflect this special historical situation.[17] Only as Quebec society assumes greater responsibility for itself is the church free to define itself anew, this time with greater self-reliance.

The double reference to past and future allowed the commission to select significant ideas and proposals from the vast material gathered by it. Disregarded were the aspirations of Catholics that express an attachment to the past without any sense of the newness that is presently demanded. Equally excluded from consideration were radical recommendations for the future unconcerned about the church's historical continuity. In the new situation the church can constitute its collective identity only if it sees itself as both a project and a heritage.

Faithful to the heritage

What precisely is the heritage to which the church as project must be faithful? The report focussed on three characteristics: i) the missionary orientation of the Quebec church, ii) its commitment to French-Canadian and later Quebec society and iii) its character as a *communio*, a communion, a community of solidarity and shared values. None of these characteristics are difficult to document. The report dwells on the extraordinary missionary engagement of the church over the centuries, which involved sending priests and religious to new regions in North America and eventually to other continents.[18] The report called to memory the church's second characteristic: its profound involvement with the French-Canadian people and its active role at all levels of French-Canadian society.[19] At one time the church believed it could speak on behalf of Quebec society. The report finally recalled the church's communal spirit: the close bonds among parishioners and between them and their parish priest; the sense of kinship, tribal cohesion and social solidarity.[20] These bonds have bound the Quebec church together over the centuries.

How does this heritage merge with the church's contemporary project? The missionary orientation, the report argued, is strongly expressed in the contemporary church's concern with what theologians call "the world." Following the spirit of Vatican Council II, the Catholics who addressed the commission had a strong sense of their mission in society and history. The church as a contemporary project seeks to serve the world. The church does not exist for itself and is not preoccupied with its own life. Instead the church bears the burdens of humanity, offers insights and help toward the humanization of society and so proclaims its message about the transcendent God.[21]

In these reflections the report followed the teaching of Vatican Council II. Thus the report recognized that the church also learns from the world. Part of the church's mission is dialogue with society, with political movements and ideas, with the social sciences and philosophical thought.

The church's traditional concern for French-Canadian society emerges in the contemporary project as the church's abiding commitment to the Quebec people.[22] Since the church now represents a minority in society, it is ready to accept pluralism and join the public debate about the common good and Quebec's cultural, political and economic orientation. Because it no longer speaks for the whole, the church is now able to exercise a socio-critical function — a prophetic role — defending the weaker members of society and calling for social and economic justice.

This section of the report echoed the theme developed in Jacques Grand'Maison's 1965 *Crise de prophétisme*, a brilliant book that anticipated a theological trend in the Christian church, identified a few years later with the political theology of the German theologian Johann-Baptist Metz. The report actually quoted from a lecture by Metz on the church's socio-critical role, given in 1970 at a theological congress held in Brussels.[23]

Most important here is the way the report depicted the church's fidelity to the third characteristic of its inheritance: its communal nature. At this point the report introduced the three themes of participation, pluralism and the toleration of dissent.[24] Because the church is a communion, the report argued, it may not be thought of as "an immutable pyramid throughout the ages nor as an inaccessible obelisk."[25] A highly centralized bureaucracy hides the church's true nature as the communion of the faithful. Communion implies participation. As the Quebec people, mobilized by the Quiet Revolution, have acquired a strong sense of their social responsibility, so have the Catholics among them developed the conviction that they have a collective responsibility for their church too. "The democratization of secular life has not failed to influence the expectations of the faithful, whether they be lay people, religious or priests."[26]

The report pointed to the teaching of Vatican II about the presence of the Spirit in the people and about the ecclesial principle of collegiality as proof that the aspirations of Quebec Catholics are in line with the emerging self-understanding of the church as a whole.

This call for democratization in no way questioned the episcopal-papal structure of the church which Roman Catholics regard as institutions *iure divino*. The report claimed that "the introduction of democratic ways can go a long way without compromising the hierarchical structure."[27] What was demanded was simply wider consultation and co-operation. The faithful and their priests want to participate in some way in the decision-making process affecting the church's pastoral message and policies. The report said that the preservation of the character of the Quebec church as communion requires the creation of certain *lieux de participation* to give a concrete form to the co-responsibility of the baptized. The report made institutional recommendations to this end.

Because of the church's heritage as communion, it should be possible to preserve solidarity among the faithful in spite of the internal pluralism. First of all, the renewal of institutions is a gradual process and affects some more quickly than others. According to the report, the church as project must affirm a certain internal pluralism. Secondly, the contemporary church's urgent concern for social justice will undoubtedly produce some pluralism among its members. There are a number of political trends offering different analyses and strategies. Some Catholics will opt for moderate solutions and others will choose more radical ones.

Finally, there exist within the church differing religious aspirations and differing theological interpretations of the principal thrust of the Gospel, all of which deserve respect. This is the third source of pluralism within the Quebec church.

The report recommended the idea that the church as project, faithful to its heritage as *communio*, should welcome a certain pluralism among Catholics. The report reminded its readers that Pius XII recognized the need for an informed public opinion in the church[28] and that, more recently, Paul VI asked Catholics to avoid "a single word" and "a single solution" in response to today's challenges.[29] The report concludeed that "one must denounce the tendency of long standing, also among lay people, to reduce the response to a complex set of problems to a single official definition, especially coming from Rome."[30] There is room in the church for responsible dissent and respectful opposition. "There exists in the church a Christian ethics of dissent, criteria of Gospel authenticity permitting protest, in fact a pluralism inscribed in the Catholic tradition, marked as it is by tensions. It is important to remind those who cling to the "letter" — to their "letter" — of the transcendent claim of the Spirit."[31]

In recommending participatory procedures in the church and in welcoming a certain pluralism, the report believed it was faithful to its principle of double reference, *l'Église: un héritage, un projet*. The commission set aside the radical proposals made by certain Catholics because these suggestions did not protect the church's historical continuity and hence its spiritual collective identity. The commission regarded its own recommendations as responsible, moderate and balanced. The report argued that the church must democratize its social existence to remain faithful to its spiritual foundation and its evangelical mission.

Structural reform

One important section of the report, dealing with church structures, made a series of institutional recommendations.[32] Here the report clarified what it meant by *lieux de participation*. The report proposed an institutional strategy along two lines: the creation at various levels of clearly defined "centres of decision making" to formulate pastoral policies and also the creation of "common assemblies" to invite the participation of people affected by the policies made in their "centre of decision making."[33]

What does this proposal mean for the parish? The report recommended the creation in all parishes of a "pastoral council" open to laymen and women and "an episodic assembly" that periodically convokes all community members to reveal their concerns, evaluate present policies, enlarge the parish's concerns and initiate new pastoral ventures.[34] Since the pastoral council is to be the decision-making body, the report suggests that the parish priest not act as a man of authority but as a "facilitator" and "team leader."

The commission debated at great length whether or not the parish itself was still a useful and viable institution.[35] Parishes in small towns and villages have retained much of their vitality. But in the big cities, especially Montreal, parishes were in trouble. Their difficulty was caused in part by the rapid secularization of the population and in part by the trend among the faithful to form smaller, more intimate and more engaging groups and to stay away from their parishes The commission eventually decided to defend the institution of the parish but recommended that the parish priest welcome the formation of smaller groups and try to be present to them. The commission recognized that the greatest vitality of a religious organization is usually found in its smaller groups, movements and networks. These formations should be encouraged, the report argued, even if they should choose to remain independent of the ecclesiastical structures, as long as their spiritual concern is in keeping with the basic orientation of the church as a whole.

The report also recommended the creation of new institutions, "pastoral zones," to bring together from different parishes people who share common concerns, common conditions or common problems. Such zones could embrace, for instance, the workers, the youth, or the unemployed and welfare recipients in large neighbourhoods or other defined areas.[36] Here the centre of decision making would be an appointed zone council, possibly made up exclusively of lay people. The common assembly would be a meeting, held at regular intervals, open to all affected by the zone's activities. The report expressed the hope that these new institutions would promote a certain de-clericalization of church ministry.

The commission recognized that Vatican Council II had already suggested the creation of parish councils and the setting up of a pastoral council or a council of priests in the diocese. These institutions were to promote collegiality, dialogue and co-operation in the church. The recommendations of the Dumont Report move in the same direction, but go far beyond the narrow limits set by ecclesiastical tradition to the effective participation of lay people.

The report proposed the creation in each diocese of a pastoral council presided over by the bishop, as the centre of decision making. It also suggested the convocation at regular intervals of a pastoral assembly to allow the people and their priests to express their concerns and propose new pastoral orientations.[37] Since the church wants to encourage the various movements in the diocese, representatives of these movements should become members of the pastoral council. This would bring them into an ongoing dialogue with the bishop and the diocese as a whole and overcome the present situation where the movements often find themselves misunderstood and subject to heavy-handed, bureaucratic decisions. If the pastoral council is allowed to assume its full responsibility, the diocesan bureaucracy, presently the locus of many arbitrary and sometimes conflicting decisions, would become an executive agent to implement the decisions of the pastoral council.

The report also made concrete proposals, following the same principle, for inter-diocesan structures and structures for the entire Quebec church.[38] Their purpose was to overcome the bureaucratic style of church government, enhance the co-operation and co-ordination of the church's pastoral projects and increase lay participation at all levels of the decision-making process.

The democratization of the church proposed by the Dumont Commission could be implemented within existing Roman Catholicism if the bishops, out of pastoral zeal and love for democratic co-operation, decided to limit the power assigned to them by canon law. At the parish level, any sharing in decision making at present depends on the generosity of the parish priest. Yet structures not written into law but dependent on good will of the powerful will be fragile and unstable. Implicit in the Dumont Report was the wish that the recommended democratization will one day be approved by the Catholic church as a whole and inscribed in a new codex of canon law.

* * *

While the Parent Report transformed the educational system in Quebec, the Dumont Report had a limited impact on the Quebec church. There were reasons for this quite apart from the reticence of some of the bishops. The secularization of Quebec culture continued throughout the seventies and eighties. The enthusiasm of engaged Catholics, produced by the reforms of Vatican II and the rapid transformation of Quebec society, had begun to wane by the time the report was published in the early seventies. During its preparation the interest of Catholics had been most intense. The high attendance and the ardent participation at the hearings organized through the province had demonstrated to the commission members the widespread, enthusiastic concern for the renewal of the Christian life. The reasons for the decline of this enthusiasm in the seventies are not examined in this chapter.

Still the Dumont Report was not without influence. The Quebec bishops, supported by a network of social justice committees, adopted a critical, prophetic stance in regard to Quebec society. In their pastoral letters the bishops criticized the economic and political orientation of contemporary society because it creates unemployment, provides jobs that are increasingly precarious, widens the gap between rich and poor and humiliates the growing crowd of welfare recipients. This critical, prophetic stance has been present especially in the bishops' collective statements. In their own dioceses, many bishops remained conservative, indifferent to the recommendations of the Dumont Report. Yet collectively the Quebec bishops have demonstrated their commitment to Quebec society in many ways. Before the referendum of 1980, while not telling Catholics whether to vote Yes or No, the bishops strongly defended Quebec's right to political self-determination.[39] The bishops may not have welcomed the growing pluralism within the Quebec church, but on the whole they have not interfered in the pastoral projects set up by Catholic groups, even when these seemed somewhat radical. While the parishes continued to decline and lose their members, especially in metropolitan Montreal, the Catholic community — now a minority — remained a place of remarkable vitality and imagination, open to new ideas and new experiments.

The attempt to democratize Catholic institutions was unsuccessful. So far all efforts to make the Catholic church a more participatory organization have failed.

At the present the policy of John Paul II, strongly supported by sections of the Roman Curia, seems to be the restoration of papal monarchy. A sociologist might argue that a religious organization widely spread in Western democratic countries will not be able to resist the trend toward democracy for long. A breakthrough will suddenly occur. Yet another sociologist might argue that the dominant trend in the democratic countries is not at all toward greater participation but, on the contrary, toward centralization and bureaucratization. Modern society is moving toward "the iron cage," as Max Weber called this trend at the beginning of the century. If this is true, then the Catholic style of ecclesiastical government seems in line with what is happening in the large national and transnational organizations. If this is true, then no democratic breakthrough is to be expected in the Catholic church. Of course one great difference between business organizations and churches is that leaving the former exacts a great price and is often almost impossible, while leaving the latter has no social burden attached to it in the present culture.

Chapter Three

"Politisés chrétiens": A Christian-Marxist Network in Quebec, 1974-1982

During the 1970s, in many parts of the world, Christians committed to social justice became actively involved in socialist movements. They joined socialist parties and organizations and supported the socialist orientation gaining ground in labour unions and other social organizations. These Christians created their own institutional networks. They did this not to set up parallel political structures but to support one another, to reflect on their new experiences and to relate their socialist commitment to the meaning of the Christian message.

Crucial for understanding Christian socialism in the seventies were the upheaval of Latin American society, the emergence of radical Catholic movements and the creation of a body of literature called liberation theology. In Chile in 1971 Christians for Socialism, an organization of priests and religious who supported Salvador Allende's Popular Unity coalition, was formed and the following year held its first convention in Santiago. This was attended by more than four hundred priests, nuns, brothers and lay people from all over Latin America. Also present were supporters from Europe and North America. The convention was an event of historic significance that encouraged the formation of Christian socialist organizations in Latin America and on other continents — although the Chilean organization itself did not survive the 1973 coup d'état.

Historical antecedents

Before turning to the impact of these events on Quebec Christians I will make two more general remarks about the formation of Christian socialism in the seventies. Even though the history of this world-wide phenomenon has not yet been written, it seems to me that the rapid spread of the movement in many parts of the world and the ready response to it in Quebec can only be understood by considering two historical developments.

The first development was sparked by Vatican Council II (1962-1965), which transformed the Catholic church's perception of the world, created an urgent sense of social responsibility, and engendered solidarity with the poor and oppressed. This social commitment was strengthened by the 1968 Latin American Bishops Conference at Medellin, Colombia, and the 1971 World Synod of Bishops held in Rome.[1] According to this Synod Christian salvation included the liberation of people from oppression; and for this reason the Gospel was not authentically proclaimed unless it was accompanied by action for social justice.[2] The church's official social teaching began to assume a distinctly progressive orientation. During the sixties a similar shift to the left occurred in the positions and policies adopted by the largely Protestant World Council of Churches, based in Geneva, Switzerland.[3]

This shift affected the Catholic bishops of Quebec and Canada. Their 1970 Labour Day message, *Liberation in a Christian Perspective*, reflected the new orientation: "Canadians who have been denied basic human needs and social influence are fed up. In 1968 the Economic Council of Canada referred to the deprived citizens as 'unwilling outsiders, virtual non-participants in society.' Since then a growing number of Canada's poor have become politically conscious and have begun to group together in order to demand participation in all policy-making which affects their lives. This is their human right."[4] Since that time the bishops of Quebec and Canada have produced several social messages that offer a critique of the present order and summon their people to engage in critical social action.

The shift of orientation in ecclesiastical teaching was itself a response on the part of church leaders to pressures exerted by the base, by Christian activist groups in third-world countries and to a lesser extent in Europe and North America. Yet the new social teaching influenced the wider Christian community. It created in the church a general climate of openness to social change.

While the church favoured an *apertura a sinistra*, Christian socialist organizations actually defined themselves in opposition to the church's new teaching. They accused the bishops of being blindly optimistic in regard to liberal society: despite their radical-sounding statements, the bishops were still expecting that social justice could be brought about incrementally within the framework of the existing order.

A second historical development which preceded the formation of Christian socialism in the seventies was the increasing mobilization of society. The mobilization of a population involves the creation of an ardent political consciousness through new ideas, public debates, artistic productions and mass demonstrations. This presupposes the existence of an organizational infrastructure, a multiple network of groups, parties and associations, bringing people together and encouraging their participation. Such conditions make a mass movement possible. Beginning in the sixties this sort of mobilization took place in different countries with varying degrees of intensity.

In the context of this broad mobilization Christian socialists in many countries defined themselves in opposition to a powerful political party that presented itself as progressive. This was true in Latin America where liberation theology and the Christian socialist organizations vehemently opposed Christian Democracy, a political movement that claimed to be a social democratic "third way" between capitalism and socialism.[5] In several European countries radical Christian organizations also made Christian Democracy the special object of their attack. Quebec's Christian radicals followed a similar path, defining themselves in opposition to the social democratic stance of the newly-formed Parti Québécois.

Both trends — a progressive climate in the church and the political mobilization of society — were strongly present in Quebec. There can be no doubt that in the sixties and seventies Quebec was a highly politicized society. After the early years of the Quiet Revolution Quebecers increasingly saw themselves as participants in a liberation movement for national self-determination. The anti-colonial struggles in Africa, the Algerian war and the civil rights movement in the United States were creating a political discourse that growing numbers of Quebecers used to define their own political and cultural endeavour. The sense of urgency was intensified by the federal government's response to the so-called October crisis of 1970.

This mobilization of society also generated an ardent social activism within the Catholic church. In the late sixties the specialized Catholic Action organizations — Jeunesse ouvrière catholique (JOC), Jeunesse étudiante catholique (JEC), Jeunesse rurale catholique

(JRC) and Mouvement des travailleurs chrétiens (MTC) — became increasingly politicized. This development worried the Quebec bishops. They created a study commission directed by the well-known sociologist, Fernand Dumont, with a mandate to recommend new directions for Catholic Action. Eventually the Dumont commission was asked to broaden its perspective, produce a critical study of the entire Quebec church and come up with proposals for the church's pastoral orientation in the new age.[6]

The mobilization of society also led to the formation of entirely new organizations in the church.[7] A special 1970 issue of the Jesuit review *Relations* titled "L'animation sociale" described the multiplication of popular organizations in Quebec and linked them with the awakening of a new collective consciousness.[8] The same issue recorded a parallel development within the church involving activist and consciousness-raising groups *(les projets d'animation)* and militant Christians working as facilitators *(les équipes d'animation)*. Many Christian base communities were formed throughout Quebec (especially in Montreal). They communicated with one another through the bulletin *Koinonia* later called *Communion*,[9] in which they clarified their ideas and debated their strategies. Yet the base communities lasted only a few years. More stable — and active to this day — was the Centre de pastoral en milieu ouvrier (CPMO), founded by the church in downtown Montreal in 1970 as a response to aspirations and pressures coming from the base.

Emergence of a Marxist movement

Many Quebec Catholics followed with great interest the radicalization of religion in Latin America, the new religious literature called liberation theology and the formation of Catholic socialist organizations in Chile and elsewhere. These developments were widely discussed among Christian activists. Eventually a group of

Quebec Christians formed their own socialist organization, the Réseau des politisés chrétiens, a network of
regional groups involving 300 to 400 members from all
parts of the province. The network was formally
founded in 1974 and dissolved in 1982.

This chapter will examine the emergence of this
organization and its ideological orientation. In this pre-
liminary study the information is mainly derived from
articles published in the Jesuit review, *Relations*, and the
Oblate review, *Prêtres et laïcs*, which after 1974 became
Vie ouvrière. I have also examined the mimeographed
books produced by the Réseau and relied on casual
conversations with friends. Members of the Réseau are
identified by name only if their names appear in public
documents.

Relations is such an important source because Yves
Vaillancourt, the initiator and one of the leading spirits
of the network, wrote for *Relations* and was a member of
its editorial committee. From 1970 to 1976 this remarkable Christian, gifted leader and dedicated researcher
was undoubtedly one of the most influential personali-
ties among the *politisés chrétiens*. He is still a productive
scholar and a man of profound conviction. Articles by
Yves Vaillancourt and other authors recorded the process leading to the formation of the Réseau. Beyond this
history, the articles described the gradual transformation of the Catholic conscience as it wrestled with the
necessity of maintaining a double fidelity — to the
Christian message and to political solidarity with the
oppressed. For Christian socialists the revolutionary
struggle was not a purely secular affair; it had a spiritual, inward dimension as a response to the divine
summons.

Yves Vaillancourt's first article in December 1970
was written under the impact of the October crisis. Here
Vaillancourt criticized the social democratic orientation
he found in the progressive political statements and
church documents of the day.[10] In May 1971 he reported

on the revolutionary Christians in Latin America.[11] In the same issue there are excerpts from *Amour chrétien et violence révolutionaire* by Jules Girardi, an Italian priest and militant socialist who argued against the church's condemnation of the class struggle.[12] He insisted that the class struggle inflicted by the powerful on the weak is present in history whether we like it or not, and that the summons to love does not allow Christians to remain neutral in this struggle but instead compels them to take sides.

In June, 1971, in his analysis of a progressive ecclesiastical document, Yves Vaillancourt acknowledged that the Quebec church had moved from a conservative to a reformist position. Yet for him this was not enough; he argued that even progressive church documents misrepresent Marxism and thus implicitly defend the existing capitalist order.[13]

The July-August 1971 issue of *Relations* presented "The Participation of Christians in the Construction of Socialism," the declaration of eighty Chilean priests in support of Chilean President Allende's Popular Unity coalition.[14] The priests claimed that Marxists increasingly understand Marxism as a sociology of oppression and a guide for political strategy and no longer as a materialistic philosophy. At the same time they noted that Christians increasingly attempt to sever their message and religious practice from an ideological identification with the established order: "The profound reason for our commitment is our faith in Jesus Christ incarnate in the historical conditions of the people." Christians, they asserted, must be in solidarity with workers and the poor, which in Chile meant support for Popular Unity.

The September 1971 issue contained Vaillancourt's article,"Un réseau á batir," which argued that a new type of Christian was being created in Quebec.[15] The consciousness-raising groups and community organizations that were radicalizing the population were led by fully engaged facilitators and organizers, many of whom were committed Christians. Because these *politisés chrétiens* constituted a minority at odds with the mainstream in church and society, it might be useful for them to build a network of mutual support. Vaillancourt invited these Christians to discuss this proposal with their local groups and report on their reactions. The pages of *Relations* would record the development of the network.

In the same month, the labour federation, Confédération des syndicats nationaux (CSN), published a working document, "Ne comptons que sur nos propres moyens," which analysed the social evolution in terms of class conflict, rejected the capitalist system and called for the construction of a socialist alternative.[16] A similar radicalization took place in the other major labour federations, the Fédération des travailleurs du Québec (FTQ) and the Centrale des enseignants du Québec (CEQ). The *politisés chrétiens* attached great importance to this development.

The January 1972 issue of *Relations* carried Yves Vaillancourt's interpretation of Quebec labour history. This view remained normative for the Réseau in the years to come.[17] Pointing to the Marxist social analysis published by the three labour federations and used in the daily practice of social organizers, Vaillancourt argued that after October 1970 the Quebec labour movement had moved from a social democratic to a Marxist-socialist orientation. Christians in solidarity with labour thus had to come to understand society in terms of class conflict on the political, cultural and ideological level.

Following Latin American Christian socialists and Jules Girardi, Vaillancourt explained in the same article that Marxism, understood as a scientific instrument, posed no difficulties for believing Christians. At the same time a Marxist analysis significantly modified the perception of Quebec's national quest for political sovereignty. This was a crucial issue for Quebecers. While he acknowledged the justice of Quebec's struggle for independence, he warned against separating it from the struggle for socialism. A nationalist movement guided by the Quebec bourgeoisie would not liberate the working class.

Vaillancourt did not lose interest in the specifically religious and spiritual dimension of the struggle. In his reflections he provided elements of a liberation theology.[18] The Christian church had become accustomed to thinking of itself as the believing community that brought the light of the Gospel to a world lying in darkness. It would be theologically more sound, Vaillancourt argued, to think of the church as the community enlightened by the Gospel that recognizes and supports the work of the Holy Spirit in history: in the historical struggle, the class struggle, for human liberation. He acknowledged the danger that an intense, political involvement could remove Christians from the evangelical ground where they stand, but this risk, the Christian risk, must be taken. The network being built, he argued, is intended to strengthen radical Christians in their faith. Solidarity with the workers' struggle would be the locus of new religious experiences.

The *politisés chrétiens*, Vaillancourt wrote, define their position in opposition to the conservative church of the past and the progressive church of the present. They recognize the class struggle as an historical movement that passes right through the church and divides the Christian community — a fact which church leaders do not want to recognize and which they disguise with an inauthentic rhetoric of unity and reconciliation. Still it would be unrealistic, Vaillancourt argued, to expect a worldwide organization such as the Catholic church to be able to extricate itself from its alliance with the dominant powers. The church as a whole would be freed only when society itself had been freed. Radical Christians should therefore not judge the church too harshly or feel called upon to leave it.

In May 1972 *Relations* reported on a meeting the previous month where the building of a network of radical Christians was discussed. Seventy participants from Chicoutimi, Drummondville, Hull, Joliette, Montreal, Quebec, Rimouski, St. Hyacinthe, Trois-Rivières, and North East Quebec had attended.[19] The participants were for the most part organizers or facilitators of Catholic Action groups in the popular sector. The problems these activists experienced and the questions they raised made the formation of a network a matter of some urgency. They decided to hold regional meetings to discuss this formation and prepare for a larger, Quebec-wide meeting that would take the final step. While the network was being built, a Montreal secretariat was already at work producing study documents on Quebec labour history and the church's relation to the workers.

A month later *Relations* published a report on the April 1972 founding convention of Christians for Socialism, in Santiago.[20] Of the 400 participants, half were from socialist Chile and the rest largely from other Latin American countries. Among them were well-known liberation theologians; Jules Girardi had come from Italy. Four Quebecers attended the convention, among them Yves Vaillancourt. *Relations* printed a French translation of the convention's final document. Many readers were surprised that this text did not adopt the social-ethical discourse of liberation theology, which emerged from a creative dialogue between scripture and political economy. Instead the document took the highly conceptual, scientific approach of Althusserian Marxism then influential at Latin American universities. Radical Quebec Christians were in doubt about this purely scientific approach. An interesting panel discussion on Marxism, organized by the Centre de pastorale en milieu ouvrier (CPMO) in September 1973 and reported in the November issue of *Prêtres et laïcs*, revealed two contrasting interpretations of Marxism.[21]

Panelist Yves Vaillancourt presented Marxism as a movement that provided the two things necessary for human emancipation: a utopia that summons forth vision and passion and a scientific method for analysing the contradictions of society and its culture. Christians derive their utopia from a different source, the divine promises revealed in Christ, but they are grateful for the scientific analysis of society in terms of infrastructure and superstructure, modes of production, forces of production and relations of production. This approach does not imply an economic determinism. The economic infrastructure determines the orientation of history only in the long run. Personal freedom plays an important part in the working out of this historical dialectic.

The second panelist, Jérôme Régnier, took a different stand by arguing that there is no one Marxist science. He defended the widely held thesis that Marxism exists in two antithetical forms: one humanist, derived from Marx's own writings and concerned with the workers' struggle to overcome alienation; the other scientific, derived largely from Engels and Lenin. Influenced by Darwinian evolutionary theory, the scientific type of Marxism regards the human struggle as the prolongation of the evolutionary struggle existing in nature and in matter itself.

The scientific approach, Régnier argued, was unable to appreciate human subjectivity. In contrast Karl Marx himself tended to analyse the primary contradiction of capitalism in human-ethical rather than purely scientific terms. He saw that the labour demanded by the new forces of production had become social, involving the many, while the ownership of the means of production was still in private hands, involving only the few. Goods produced by the many were expropriated by the few. Marx regarded this as outrageous. The class struggle he depicted aimed at the emancipation of the workers and through them of the whole society.

Régnier recommended a humanist social analysis that paid greater attention to the subjective factors.

The Réseau eventually adopted the scientific approach discussed and defended by Yves Vaillancourt. Yet the panel discussion revealed a conflict that remained alive in the Christian left and eventually surfaced among the members of the Réseau.

Building the network

Building the network of *politisés chrétiens* in Quebec was a slow process. The Réseau finally was launched in April 1974 with a membership of several hundred.[22] The direction was in the hands of a co-ordinating committee, with four or five members. Two commissions were set up, one concerned with political analysis and the other with theological reflection. The commissions' tasks were assigned by the co-ordinating committee. The members of the Réseau, scattered over Quebec's various regions, communicated through messages and papers sent by the co-ordinating committee, through regional meetings and occasionally through national assemblies. These assemblies were not decision-making bodies. Decisions about the correct analysis of the historical situation, the political strategy to be pursued, and the topics to be studied by the commissions were made by the co-ordinating committee in consultation with the members. The Réseau's organization was formal and disciplined, reflecting the Catholic institutional tradition as well as the "democratic centralism" of more recent origin.

The documents and papers produced by the Réseau and studied by its members were mimeographed, rather than printed and published. In them the Réseau defined its function, presented its social analysis and communicated the line that members should pursue in the labour organizations and popular groups to which they belonged. In these documents and papers the

Réseau also explained what God's revelation in Jesus Christ meant to them, the place this divine revelation held in the struggle for human liberation, and how the members should relate themselves to their church and its institutions.

The Réseau was not involved in political action and did not conceive political action as one of its functions. Rather it saw itself as a support group for Christian Marxists with a political mission in the field of culture and ideology. The *politisés chrétiens* believed that in this area they could make a special contribution to the struggle for socialism. It is worth noting that the Réseau also had Protestant members. Demographic conditions meant that Catholics were the great majority, yet they were ecumenical from the beginning and welcomed Protestant comrades.

The "First Document," in which the newly founded Réseau defined itself, published in the November 1974 *Relations*, gave a precise account of how the network understood the political situation of Quebec society and the role of *politisés chrétiens* within it.[23] The analysis began with an examination of the evolution of the Quebec labour movement since 1960. From 1960 to 1965 labour participated in the Quiet Revolution promoted by the Liberal Party (PLQ), student activists, progressive artists and intellectuals. Here the state took the initiative and used its power to develop Quebec society. This process led to new jobs in government offices, schools, hospitals and social service, thus creating a new class of nationalist petit bourgeois. In the second stage from 1966 to 1969, labour became more critical of government policy and turned to social democracy as defined by René Lévesque and elements in the emerging Parti Québécois (PQ). In the third stage from 1970 to 1974, labour recognized that the new nationalism had the support of the rising Quebec bourgeoisie intent on replacing the English Canadian bourgeoisie. The major labour federations, radicalized by the 1970 October crisis, became critical of the capitalist economy and begin to turn to socialism. What had taken place, the Réseau believed, was a qualitative change.

The "First Document" presented an analysis of labour's position in 1974. It named the labour organizations that were still only nationalist, others that were social democratic — though some of their leaders were having serious doubts — and finally it named the labour organizations whose leaders were becoming revolutionary socialists. The Réseau saw the movement of history in this turn to socialism. The important remaining work was to support this movement by persuading the workers who were questioning the present system to turn to socialism.

The Réseau members called themselves *politisés*, not socialists. At the first international convention of Christians for Socialism in 1975 at Cap-Rouge, Quebec, attended by 400 participants from all parts of the world, the *politisés chrétiens* explained why they had not joined this international organization and why they had not adopted the same title for their own network.[24] The reason was that Quebec workers had not yet come to think of themselves as socialists, despite the conversion to socialism by many of their leaders. The *politisés chrétiens* did not wish to rush ahead of the workers in this regard.

The social analysis of the "First Document" distinguished two fundamental classes: the capitalists (the bourgeoisie) and the workers (the proletariat) and recognized an intermediary class (the petite bourgeoisie), whose allegiance is not clearly defined. The traditional petite bourgeoisie was identified as the old leadership of Quebec society, the modern petite bourgeoisie as the emerging class that supports modernization and industrialization of Quebec society and the revolutionary petite bourgeoisie as the radical intellectuals and artists who have opted for socialism. Finally there was the semi-proletariat — poor people, welfare recipients and others on the margins.

The *politisés chrétiens* did not use these categories in a purely rhetorical fashion. They used them as scientific instruments of social analysis. In subsequent documents and in their books they repeatedly refined these categories — in this they drew upon the work of Nicos Poulantzas whom they highly regarded — and they used the categories to study the transformation of Quebec society, past and present. The Réseau inspired its academically trained, intellectual members to dedicate their time to historical, sociological and theological research.

Already the "First Document" revealed how the Réseau understood its mission in Quebec. This understanding was shaped by the social analysis it had adopted. In this analysis the two fundamental classes, the bourgeoisie and the proletariat, have an historical orientation defined by their relation to production. They are the participants in a class struggle that will eventually lead to the establishment of socialism. At this time the nature of the struggle is still obscure in the minds of many workers. The petite bourgeoisie, on the other hand, is not directly connected with the process of production. Since its role is not defined by historical forces, it has a class option. Members of the petite bourgeoisie, especially intellectuals, teachers, social workers, church employees and clerics, are capable of acting in solidarity with the working class movement. Their intellectual and cultural activity can help remove the ideological obstacles that prevent so many workers from recognizing the class struggle and also persuade many members of the petite bourgeoisie to shift their loyalty to the workers.

This analysis presupposes that personal freedom, especially among the intermediary classes and the workers, plays an important role in the historical process which in the long run is determined by economic factors. It also emphasizes the important contribution that Christians can make to the socialist movement in Quebec. Many Quebec workers were afraid of revolutionary socialist organizations, partly because of the church's prior condemnation of socialism. The Réseau believed that workers might become less suspicious and more open if they met socialists who were good, believing Catholics. The network also wanted to persuade believing Christians in the intermediate classes that fidelity to Jesus necessitated solidarity with the oppressed and a class option in favour of the proletariat.

Finally, the *politisés chrétiens* had a special role to play among the welfare poor and low income people, designated as the semi-proletariat. Often forgotten by organized labour, this class was an important focus of church involvement: this class could well become politicized through the activity of socialist Christians living in the poor neighbourhoods. The *politisés chrétiens* believed that as Christians they could help the socialist movement by expanding its social base to include a wider spectrum of the population.

To facilitate their work among the people the *politisés chrétiens* kept on studying theology. The coordinating committee distributed to the members important articles dealing with liberation theology in Latin America and comparable trends in the European Christian left. The commission charged with theological reflection prepared a mimeographed book, *Pour une intelligence révolutionnaire de la foi,* which applied the principles of liberation theology to the Quebec situation.

In the Quebec of the seventies traditional Catholic ideology was a minor obstacle to socialism. The greater ideological obstacle, according to the Réseau, was the illusory ideal of social democracy. Many workers and social critics in the intermediate classes were caught up in the reformist project of social democracy. So too was the church, as evidenced by its new progressive teaching. These groups supported the Parti Québécois.

The *politisés chrétiens* took their intellectual struggle against social democracy and its representative, the Parti Québécois, very seriously. Studying the political and economic history of Canada, the academics among them tried to show that social democratic reforms, introduced by whatever political party, had always improved the economic situation of the bourgeoisie more than that of the exploited working class. The Réseau commission charged with political analysis prepared a mimeographed book, *La social-démocratie et les militants chrétiens.* Demonstrating first of all that the majority of progressive Catholic organizations had adopted a social democratic perspective in the seventies, the book then argued that this ideology was an obstacle to socialism and that Réseau members should work against this trend in the Catholic organizations where they belonged.

Throughout its existence the Réseau remained faithful to the perspective and the analysis embraced from the very beginning. The Réseau continued to believe that after 1970 Quebec workers were moving toward revolutionary socialism. The network continued to refine its class analysis and review the concrete *conditions* of society *(la conjoncture)* to determine members' strategies in their various organizations.

In the nationalist debate the Réseau followed the perspective articulated in Yves Vaillancourt's January 1972 article on Quebec labour history.[25] These radical Christians were nationalists who viewed Quebecers as a people with an unalienable right to self-determination. They became *indépendantistes* because they believed it would be easier to create a socialist Quebec than a socialist Canada due to the greater politicization of Quebec labour. Yet they had many hesitations regarding Quebec nationalism because they mistrusted the Parti Québécois and opposed its social democratic vision of a sovereign Quebec. Members of the Réseau kept in contact with socialists of their stripe in English Canada. While their position during the referendum debate was Yes, but . . . , they still voted Yes.

The impact of the Réseau on the Quebec church must have been considerable. In 1977 a progressive pastoral letter of the Canadian bishops contained a warning against Marxist influence among Christian activists:"Some Christians, longing for justice and equality, trying to free present-day society from its idols and to change human relationships, seek to harmonize Marxism with the Gospel. There are however great dangers in this undertaking."[26]

The pastoral letter urged Christians to grasp the social imperative implicit in the Gospel and become politically involved. But how? Excluded on ethical grounds were both the simple defence of the status quo and the promotion of a Marxist alternative. The pastoral recognized with approval that: "Some Christians choose to continue reforming our present capitalist system in the light of the Gospel, and others choose to participate in socialist movements, trying to reconcile them with the teaching of Jesus."[27] Socialism was no longer taboo for Catholics.

Yet since the *politisés chrétiens* defined their position against the church's official teaching, they understood the pastoral as a reprimand addressed to them. They defended themselves by arguing that the verdict of the bishops was based on an excessively narrow, deterministic and hence incorrect understanding of Marxism.

Despite their aversion to Marxism, the Catholic bishops did not use their power to control the divergent trends in the sixties and seventies. The Quebec church had become pluralistic.[28] In 1976 the Jesuit superiors objected to the socialist orientation taken by the review, *Relations*, and expelled the radicals, including Yves

Vaillancourt, from the editorial board. Members of the Réseau found sometimes that they were no longer invited by church groups that had previously been friendly. Yet apart from public pronouncements and private remarks, the bishops did not interfere directly with the Réseau.

Conflict and decline

From the beginning the Réseau had its critics among the Catholic left. The differing views on Marxist analysis expressed at the Centre de pastorale (CPMO) panel discussion in September 1973 were an indication of this. Shortly after its foundation, in November 1974, the Réseau participated at a meeting on the topic of church and labour, organized by the CPMO at Cap-Rouge, Quebec and attended by several Catholic groups and networks identified with workers and workers' concerns. Again the participants disagreed on the use of Marxist social analysis.[29] Articles published between 1976 and 1979 in *Vie Ouvrière*, a publication close to the CPMO, and in *Relations*, show that many left-wing Christians believed that the orientation and the analysis of the Réseau were defective.

A question repeatedly asked was whether the commitment to the proletariat generated sufficient concern for the poor, for Native peoples, for unorganized workers in badly paid and insecure jobs, injured workers, the unemployed, welfare recipients, immigrants, the aged and the handicapped.[30] Was "semi-proletariat" an appropriate category? Should this "popular sector" be politicized so that it would support the class struggle of the proletariat? Or should this sector also have its own agenda?

Christian women asked similar questions. Did the class analysis of the Réseau take into consideration the double oppression inflicted on working women and poor women? In 1976 a group of politicized Catholic women constituted the collective L'autre Parole and began to publish a bulletin of that name while remaining loyal to the Réseau.[31] The collective survived the Réseau's demise and still published its bulletin in the early nineties.

A 1977 article by Raymond Levac, an activist associated with the CPMO, raised another critical issue.[32] Were Quebec workers really moving toward revolutionary socialism? Or were the perceptions of certain militant workers excessively influenced by groups of radical intellectuals? This petite bourgeoisie *radicalisée*, Levac argued, is not reliable. It tends to underestimate the insights emerging from the workers' own practical experience, often embraces Marxism in an inflexible, doctrinaire or theological manner, and provides no critique of the existing Marxisms in eastern Europe.

Critics of the Réseau's social analysis recognized that economic class was not the only factor that defined people's location — their power or powerlessness — in society. Without mentioning his name, these critics assented to Max Weber's contention that in addition to class, certain cultural factors, summed up in the word "status," also determine people's location in society. The oppression experienced by women, Native people, welfare recipients and immigrant workers derived from the low status assigned to them, not exclusively from their relationship to the means of production.

The debate of these questions led engaged Christians toward greater solidarity with the low status sectors of Quebec society. This tendency was reinforced by trends within the Latin American church. In the August 1979 issue of *Relations*, Karl Lévêques described the formation of *une église populaire*, a church of the people, in certain Latin American countries [33] and André Myre outlined the beginnings of a similar development in Quebec.[34] In Latin America Christians at the base — poor people in rural and urban situations, inspired by their faith in Christ the Liberator and often guided by radical priests — were forming collectives or communities where they resisted the worldly powers that oppressed them and where they prayed, re-read the Gospel and re-thought their Catholic faith.

This popular church did not define itself against the official church, nor did it see itself as a parallel religious organization. It understood itself rather as the locus of the church's renewal and rebirth. In public declarations the Latin American bishops themselves had endorsed "the preferential option for the poor." The bishops publicly acknowledged that the entire church was in need of conversion to a new perspective from below, a perspective which would be in solidarity with the poor and oppressed.[35] This encouraged the expectation that in and through the popular church — the church of the people — the whole church would experience the renewal of its faith and enter into solidarity with the political struggle for liberation.

In his article Karl Lévêques posed the question: Who will found *une église populaire* in Quebec? Lévêques, who was closely associated with the Réseau, realized very well that to speak of "the people" instead of "the working class" was to transcend classical Marxist theory. The promotion of a popular church would demand a new, modified theoretical orientation. The concept of socialism would have to be redefined.

The idea of a popular church assumed great importance among Quebec Catholics in 1979. In February the organization Chrétiens pour une église populaire was founded in Quebec City to promote a popular church, "a church where workers have their place and their say, a church close to the marginalized, a church that gives women their rightful place, a church involved in society standing against oppression and exploitation."[36] In May 1979, the CPMO organized a well-attended meeting at the Collège Marie-Victorin in Montreal that dealt with the promotion of the popular church in Quebec.[37]

A double imperative emerged in these discussions: first of all that the entire church be in solidarity with workers and the marginalized and secondly, that workers and the marginalized enter into solidarity among themselves. It is part of the church's pastoral mission among these various groups to raise their consciousness and promote their self-organization. Since building a network of solidarity among diverse groups is an effort that demands time and patience, the militant Christians involved with these groups are likely to have different perspectives depending on the location of their group. Unity of orientation among organized labour, unorganized workers and the various low status groups is not the beginning but the end of such a process. What emerged here was a more pluralistic understanding of the political left.

It is important to note, however, that this new trend did not represent a turn to political liberalism. It did not entertain — with Max Weber — a pluralistic understanding of society, according to which government ruled society by mediating among the different classes and sectors, all with their own distinctive interests. On the contrary these Christians looked upon their society as deeply divided, ruled in the interest of the dominant class which keeps subordinate an oppressed sector (not an economic class) made up of exploited workers and the growing ranks of the marginalized. Some considered this view of society as torn by conflict their heritage from Marxism. These Christians held that the intermediate sectors of society, where most of them belonged, were free to choose solidarity with the poor and the oppressed in their struggle for justice. At the same time they were greatly concerned that the exploited and the marginalized should experience human community, mutual support, friendship and trust in their political struggle despite their situations of deprivation. These groups would in some way anticipate what a more just, sane and close-knit society would be like.

This concern for human community may be an expression of specifically Catholic values. If this is labelled "church populism," it should be recognized that it is a decidedly left-wing populism.

It is my impression that in the late seventies the movement toward a popular church created tensions within the Réseau. Then came the loss of the referendum in 1980, followed by the political and cultural demobilization of Quebec. The Réseau co-ordinating committee continued its work as before, but participation of the members tended to decline. In 1982, after a long discussion involving members and friends — at which I was present — the co-ordinating committee decided to dissolve the network. One of the reasons for this decision was undoubtedly the re-orientation of the Catholic left toward the building of a popular church.

Chapter Four

Jacques Grand'Maison: Prophecy and Politics

Jacques Grand'Maison is a major intellectual figure in the Quebec church: a priest schooled in theology and political science, a prolific and eloquent author who has faithfully decade after decade addressed Quebec society on the important issues affecting the historical destiny of his people. This work demands intelligence, passion, perseverance and courage. Grand'Maison is a Quebec phenomenon, perhaps similar to two well-known priests of divergent theological and political orientations, Lionel Groulx and Georges-Henri Lévesque, who in the past had exercised long ministries of public criticism and political reflection. When Jacques Grand'Maison began his ministry Quebec had become a rapidly changing society and the church a rapidly changing religious community. In this new context Grand'Maison continued a certain Quebec tradition.

In this chapter I will formulate and then answer three questions about the role of ideology in Father Grand'Maison's thought. These questions are: 1) Where does Grand'Maison stand in the political spectrum of

Quebec politics? Who are his allies? For whom does he speak? 2) What does he mean by ideology? Is he only critical of ideologies, or does he promote an ideology himself? 3) What is the political meaning of his constant call for civic virtue? Is he an old-fashioned ecclesiastical moralizer who weakens people's trust in political action? Or is his call for *metanoia* part of an innovative political project?

I suppose I could have interviewed Grand'Maison and asked him how he would reply to the three questions. But I did not wish to do this. I wanted to base myself on his published work. Texts brought into the public arena communicate meanings that are no longer under the author's control; texts may even reveal messages of which the author is not fully conscious. I have turned therefore to Jacques Grand'Maison's books to find the answer to my three questions.

Where does Jacques Grand'Maison stand?

I found it difficult to reply to the first question. Grand'Maison seemed to be critical in all directions. He made scathing critiques of the change in attitudes among people engaged in changing society. People's original generous impulses were from the beginning marked by desires to improve their own situations; and as time went on and they achieved a certain success, their desires to improve their own lot and gain economic security slowly became their dominant driving force. In his social analyses Grand'Maison attaches enormous importance to the attitudes of the actors.

In his *La nouvelle classe et l'avenir du Québec* (1979)[1] he offered a devastating critique of the new middle class that effected the Quiet Revolution and so acquired power, status and high salaries in the new Quebec. Who are these "beneficiaries of the Quiet Revolution" as Grand'Maison called them? He mentioned three groups: public sector employees, intellectuals (professionals, journalists, artists) and labour union executives. He accused the people who have become successful in the new Quebec of forming a new elite preoccupied with its own security and increasingly indifferent to ordinary working people, the unemployed and the growing sector of people on welfare. Is Grand'Maison, readers ask themselves, a man of the left?

In his *Au seuil critique d'un nouvel âge* (1979),[2] based on a series of articles published in *Le Devoir* in the summer of 1978, he engaged in vehement polemics against the left and the right in Quebec. What was this left he attacked so vigorously? It consisted of small political parties, networks and groups — numerous in the seventies — guided by Marxist or neo-Marxist ideas, supported by teams of intellectuals, and inspired by the hope of building a socialist Quebec. His vehement polemic, written with passion and incisiveness, uncovered the weaknesses of these socialist formations, denounced their internal contradictions and accused their promoters of being stupid, stubborn, elitist, and uncaring about ordinary people.

In equally merciless prose Grand'Maison also attacked the right, which he defined as the "neo-liberal" cultural and political trends, powerful in England and the United States, that were making inroads in Quebec society. He denounced the recent turn to monetarism or economic liberalism with its attendant cultural consequences: increasing individualism, utilitarianism and consumerism. He complained that the successful middle class was allowing a growing sector of society to fall into unemployment, poverty and helplessness.

Catholics on the left were deeply hurt by Grand'Maison's articles in *Le Devoir*. It seemed to them that he had adopted "the ideology of the centre" often favoured by the Catholic church. The church frequently looks to the left and to the right, analyses their respective shortcomings and then presents itself as the sane and stable centre where the constructive ideas of the left and the right are preserved and put into practice. Yet the ideology of the centre abstracts from the existing power relations in society. This ideology looks upon the left and the right as if they were two equal forces without recognizing the fundamental difference in power the two actually exercise in society. The ideology of the centre wants to pick the good ideas — the raisins — from the socialist tradition without appreciating that these ideas became viable because people fought for them, confronted the powerful, made enormous sacrifices, took many risks, went to prison and often exhausted themselves.

But Grand'Maison is *not* a man of the centre. In other contexts he passionately defends what he calls "communitarian counter-structures."[3] His bitter attack was disappointing because he spoke to the left simply as an outsider. He could very well have drawn his articulate critique of the existing left from principles that properly belonged to the best insights of the left. Then he might even have been heard.

Grand'Maison, for example, argued that it was utterly unrealistic to hope for the success of a socialist party and the creation of a socialist Quebec because there existed no local socialist culture among the Quebec people. Grand'Maison could well have presented this point as an insight derived from the experiences of socialist movements. It is quite true that socialism had no popular roots in Quebec. Why? Because the Catholic church prior to Vatican II and the Quiet Revolution had expressly condemned socialism, even in its moderate forms. In contrast, socialism in the British tradition created in Saskatchewan local cultures of workers and farmers that in the thirties became the popular base of the Co-operative Commonwealth Federation (C.C.F.). If Grand'Maison had not chosen to speak as an outsider, he might well have proposed that sound socialist policy in Quebec would demand the patient effort to be close to ordinary working people and co-operate with them in laying the foundation for a popular socialist culture.

Instead Grand'Maison preferred to offer his critique of the left not as a person in basic solidarity with the labour movement and the socialist tradition. Catholics on the left found this hard to understand, especially since the more recent Catholic social teaching, especially the pastoral letters of the Quebec bishops, had appealed to Catholics of all classes to extend their solidarity to labour organizations in their struggle for a more just social order.

It occurred to me at one point that *Au seuil critique d'un nouvel âge,* published in 1979, might possibly have been written to promote the cause of the Parti Québécois (P.Q.) among the left, more especially among the Catholic left. Grand'Maison's attack against the left was aimed at Marxist groups and parties, including radical Catholic networks, who rejected the P.Q.'s social democratic platform; his polemic against the neo-liberal right was aimed at the supporters of the Quebec Liberal Party with its monetarist agenda. Yet I found nothing in the book to suggest that he was actually in solidarity with the P.Q. and spoke on its behalf. Grand'Maison's vehement critique of the new, neo-nationalist middle class, "the beneficiaries of the Quiet Revolution," in his *La nouvelle classe et l'avenir du Québec* ruled out the possibility that he identified with the P.Q.

Grand'Maison's constant and unwavering concern has been with the people at the bottom: the working poor, the unemployed, the welfare recipients, the old, the handicapped. He stood with them. He lamented that the leaders of labour unions and Marxist intellectuals were indifferent to the most powerless sector of society. Grand'Maison urged the creation of what he called "communitarian counter-structures" in this sector.

Instead of pleading with the labour movement to recognize its historical vocation in industrial society and extend its concern to the poor and the powerless (as John Paul II did in his *Laborem exercens*[4]), Grand'Maison seemed to define his solidarity with the poor in opposition to organized labour and socialism in Quebec. Many Catholics were puzzled by this.

In the eighties, encouraged by *Laborem exercens* (1981), the Canadian bishops supported the effort from various quarters to create a solidarity movement in Canada embracing progressive church groups, labour unions, the woman's movement, popular organizations and groups of the disadvantaged people. A witness to this effort was the joint declaration of 1987, *A Time to Stand Together: A Time for Social Solidarity.*[5]

Where, I asked myself, did Grand'Maison stand? Who were his allies and for whom did he speak? Important in my inquiry were two books, his autobiographical reflections, *Au mitan de la vie* (1976)[6] and one of his very first works, *Crise de prophétisme*, published in 1965.[7] In *Au mitan de la vie* Grand'Maison gave a persuasive account of his early love for freedom, his resistance to domestication and his effort to break out. As a student in Paris he had the great joy of discovering in existentialist philosophy an intellectual foundation for his own spiritual quest. From then on he would resist any closed system of ideas, political or religious. The way of truth is one of breakthrough and adventure. Grand'Maison believed that the Catholic tradition was not threatened by this approach. On the contrary resistance to domestication and the search for new frontiers made Catholicism a vital religious culture capable of self-renewal.

In his autobiography Grand'Maison discussed with great enthusiasm the famous story told by the American, Richard Bach, titled *Jonathan Livingston Seagull*. The Quebec theologian regarded this story as a magnificent poetic paradigm imaging the quest for truth and salvation. Grand'Maison discovered himself in the tamed seagull that protests against the boredom of conformity and the confinement of uncritical existence by flying to the heights and joining the wild, non-domesticated birds. Through them the seagull experiences spiritual liberation. When, in Bach's story, the liberated seagull returns to the colony of the tamed birds to tell them about his breakthrough, adventure and liberation, no one listens to him. He is rejected.

Grand'Maison here revealed himself as something of a loner. Because he has been critical in all directions, he has often marched alone. He has always been deeply involved in pastoral projects and co-operative secular endeavours in his town of St. Jerome. But, according to his own account, he remained the critic in these groups, challenging not only the policies but also and especially the attitudes of people: their growing self-preoccupation and increasing indifference to outsiders. Grand'Maison does not easily identify himself with a movement, an organization or a political party. He fears the closed system and yearns for the open project. When he writes he does not speak for any one group. He speaks in his own name for the entire Quebec people. He follows the route of the prophet who only too often walks alone.

I regard Grand'Maison's *Crise de prophétisme* as an important theological study which in 1965 was ahead of its time. In Europe and North America Catholics tended to interpret the Vatican Council as an expression of the church's new openness to liberal society, to political democracy, freedom of religion, cultural pluralism and personal development. Catholics saw the church as the spiritual community which enabled them to pursue their own journey to God and explore their own as yet unrealized potentialities.

Grand'Maison read Vatican II differently. He read the conciliar documents in the context of Quebec's Quiet Revolution. He shared with the above-mentioned interpreters the emphasis on freedom. Vatican II, Grand'Maison insisted, recognized the twofold action of the Holy Spirit among the bishops and among the faithful. The church was guided by hierarchy and by charismatic gifts. Life in the church was not an exercise of obedience to pope and bishops, but an exercise of fidelity to the Spirit. In fact the church was in great need of the original responses made by individual Christians to the Word of God.

New in Grand'Maison's interpretation was the idea that what the Spirit calls forth in Christians is a judgment on their society. Concentrating on certain passages of *Gaudium et spes*, he argued that the Gospel is truly incarnate in history; it deals with the transformation of life in society; it provides critical guidance for building a society in keeping with the biblical vision. The Gospel is misunderstood if it is read simply as an offer of personal salvation and sanctification. The biblical message is addressed to persons in the concrete historical conditions of their lives. This is the urgent message uttered by the Old Testament prophets and by New Testament heirs to this prophetic tradition, especially Jesus himself. To be prophet means precisely this: to judge your society in the light of God's word and God's promises.

All Christians, Grand'Maison insisted, are meant to be prophets. According to the conciliar teaching they participate in Christ's prophetic office through faith and baptism. What follows from this is that the Christian vocation has a political dimension. The gifts of the Spirit make the believers into social critics. They must utter the truth about their social world.

Grand'Maison proposed this idea in 1965. Since that time, the prophetico-political vocation of the Christian has been developed at length by Political Theology, beginning with Johann-Baptist Metz and Jürgen Moltmann in Germany, and by Liberation Theology, a Latin American movement of intellectual and social praxis. In 1965 Grand'Maison was clearly ahead of his time. In his book, he argued that the entire church has a prophetic mission. He believed that the church's pastoral approach, catechetical instructions, public worship and spiritual counseling should make the faithful realize their social responsibility and foster in them the spirit of prophecy.

What *Crise de prophétisme* did, quite apart from its stated purpose, was define the religious identity of Grand'Maison himself. The spiritual call to prophecy and the existentialist option here go hand in hand. He saw himself as prophet for his Québécois people, critical in all directions, evaluating the signs of the times and urging the people to move in the direction of justice, compassion and solidarity. Grand'Maison would be prophet, even if this meant being a loner.

What does Grand'Maison understand by ideology?

I found it much easier to answer the second question. In his books Grand'Maison has often spoken about ideologies. The word even got into one of his book titles, *Stratégies sociales et nouvelles idéologies.*[8] In my opinion Grand'Maison has employed the concept of ideology very much as it is used in Catholic social teaching.

Certain ideologies must simply be rejected by this teaching. If an ideology (here called ideology 1) is defined as a set of ideas that offers a rational account of the course and the meaning of history, it is for theological reasons wholly unacceptable. Since human history is the locus of a divine mystery, the mystery of redemption, the key for the understanding of history is not in the hands of scientists and philosophers. This key, Christians believe, is hidden in God. More than that, if a scientific theory could give an adequate account of the social evolution of humanity, the course of history would be determined. But Christians reject deterministic explanations of human history — including Social Darwinism and scientific Marxism. Christians argue on theological grounds that history always remains open to human agency, both to sins that corrupt and destroy, and to actions prompted by grace that overcome injustice and foster solidarity and reconciliation.

Ideologies of the first type give rise to dogmatism. Since ideologues think they know what will happen and what things mean, they will not listen to people and wrestle with the empirical data. According to John Paul II, ideologies 1 easily become idolatries, proclamations of an absolute, in the service of which it is permissible to manipulate human beings and deprive them of their human rights.

However ideologies can also be defined in a more restricted manner (here called ideologies 2) as sets of ideas that outline a social project, appeal to the imagination, mobilize people and make possible the political organization of a party or movement. Their proponents make no claim to predict the course of history. According to Catholic social teaching (and Grand'Maison has seemed to agree) such ideologies are in principle acceptable. What needs to be evaluated is whether the social project in question actually promotes social justice. Ideologies of this kind (ideologies 2) are useful and even necessary for the reconstruction of society, but they are always partial and tentative, based on a particular perception of society that may turn out to be incomplete and in need of correction. Catholic social teaching (and Grand'Maison) warn us of the danger that advocates of ideologies 2 forget their limitations and place them in the role of ideologies 1 possibly without full awareness of their action. This is how a church document puts it: "In themselves ideologies have a tendency to absolutize the interests they uphold, the vision they propose, and the strategy they promote. If this happens, they become secular religions."[9]

In the past the Catholic church has given tentative support for ideologies of the second kind, e.g. for Corporatism during the great depression and for Christian Democracy after the second world war. In Brazil and some other areas of Latin America, Catholic bishops and their dioceses have adopted Liberation Theology as a set of ideas summing up a new social project and motivating a social struggle, in other words as an ideology 2. In the 1979 Puebla Document the bishops conference denounced the ideologies 1 current in Latin America,[10] but the conference also defended the political necessity for ideologies of the second type.[11]

The Catholic church claims that its official social teaching is not an ideology either in the first or second sense, but instead is a set of social ethical principles or, more recently, a critical method to evaluate the ethical implications of a given social order.[12] In fact Catholic social teaching has often been used as an ideology. This is not surprising because people identified with a political movement, a party or a social philosophy are never totally free of ideology in the second sense. Their social project becomes the lens through which they see the social world and the norm by which they evaluate contemporary events. What is important from an ethical perspective is that people keep on testing whether the social cause they endorse (or the status quo they defend) continues to serve justice.

Very often "small l" liberals, people in basic sympathy with the present economic and political order, believe that they are free of ideology and that the left, the critics of capitalism, are ideologically tainted. Conversely this latter group sees the liberals as the people with an ideologically distorted perception of social reality. It is reported that in a public debate in Latin America about which church groups are affected by ideological thinking, a bishop proposed, "Let him who is without ideology throw the first stone."

Individuals and groups critical of ideologies often have their own ideological perspective. I am inclined to argue that this is not true for Jacques Grand'Maison. As a prophet he has shunned ideologies. He recognized the importance of second type ideologies and has realized the need for a bold, progressive, egalitarian ideology in the struggle of the Quebec people for a just and compassionate society. Yet his existentialist impatience with programs, systems and clearly defined boundaries — his vocation as "wild seagull" — has made it almost impossible for him to identify himself with a political movement or a political party. He has involved himself in important local projects at St. Jerome based on co-operatism and worker-ownership, but he has shied away from making the theoretical principles of these projects the basis of an ideology for the whole Quebec society. In his writings he has indicated the direction in which Quebec society ought to move and described the social dynamics through which such changes could occur, but his strong sense of the provisional and his keen awareness that all social projects depend on the attitudes or virtues of the participants have prevented him from identifying himself with an ideology.

Grand'Maison has a vision of a just, participatory and humane society, and he promotes clearly defined social values and attitudes, but he is unwilling to endorse an ideology. He even refuses to present himself as a man of the left. He realizes that his ideological aloofness is criticized by some of his brothers and sisters in the church who greatly admire him. He certainly knew that the articles in *Le Devoir* attacking the left emergent in Quebec society would offend many people inside and outside the church who looked upon him as a comrade. But as the wild seagull, as political existentialist, Grand'Maison was willing to bear this burden and this pain. As a prophet faithful to his call he shuns ideologies.

What is the political meaning of Grand'Maison's preaching?

Grand'Maison's writings have a high moral tone. They often contain long and detailed critiques of people's attitudes, their self-seeking, their elitism, their compulsive love of security, their indifference to the well-being of others, their lack of social solidarity, their conformity and their laziness. Grand'Maison is a preacher. My impression is that this Quebec theologian is keenly aware of the impact people's attitudes, virtues and vices have on social structures in which they live, but he is much less sensitive to the impact of these structures on personal consciousness. I have heard critics of Grand'Maison refer to his theoretical approach as "attitudinalism." Is such a criticism justified?

According to Catholic social teaching the reconstruction of society involves both structural change and ethical conversion. In the words of Pius XI, "Two things are necessary: the reform of institutions and the correction of morals."[13] But what is the relation between these two dimensions? Until fairly recently, eccesiastical teaching demanded that people at all levels of society — owners and workers — be converted to greater virtue so that, once converted, they would be able to agree on the necessary transformation of structures. The right order was, first, ethical *metanoia* and then, institutional change.

This social teaching was one of the arguments used by the magisterium against the class struggle advocated by socialists to transform institutions: socialists, the magisterium argued, had nothing to say about ethics. Against socialists and liberals, the church defended the organic model of society, with its members united by common values and common symbols. From this perspective the conflict between workers and owners could only be overcome if both groups were converted to greater justice and then, from the new vantage point, created new socio-economic institutions, the famous "corporations."

To this day Christian Democratic governments argue against the class struggle in the same way. They claim that if capitalists and working people adopt the ethical perspective presented by Christian Democracy, they will both unite in the same political movement, assured that their best interests will be protected.

This "moralism" of the older Catholic social teaching has been vehemently criticized by many Catholics struggling for social justice. They argue that preaching and pleading for conversion to greater virtue actually weakens the collective will of a people to engage in political action and to change social structures. In other words, this "moralizing" stabilizes the status quo.

More recent church teaching, disseminated in Latin America and subsequently endorsed by John Paul II, defines the relation between structural change and ethical conversion in a different way. The Latin American bishops were the first to abandon the organic view of society, until then defended by the magisterium. The organic view did not make sense in Latin American countries where the great majority were "the poor" almost totally excluded from the wealth of society. What was needed for social transformation was that the poor themselves become conscious of their political potential and wrestle for structural change, supported by all who love justice including the church. Here the call for structural change comes first. In his *Laborem exercens*, John Paul II has adopted a similar perspective. He has argued that, in the capitalist and communist countries of the north, the historical agent of social transformation — defined by him as "the priority of labour over capital" — is the labour movement, conscious of its vocation in western history and deserving the support of all who love justice. Thus John Paul II called for "the solidarity of labour and with labour."[14]

This perspective sees structural change coming first, but it in no way neglects ethical conversion. The ethic now called for is one of solidarity, a moral commitment that intensifies and guides the political struggle. Solidarity must guide the working class to become united in a common effort; solidarity must inspire the workers to take on the concerns of the poor and the unemployed; solidarity must prompt the rest of the population, including the church, to stand with and support the workers' movement for the reconstruction of society. This call for greater virtue is not moralism. It does not postpone social and political action until the conversion of the heart has occurred. Here the preaching of values aims at making the political struggle more effective.

A look at contemporary church documents shows that they are not free of a certain ambiguity. There are still certain texts, especially sermons, that offer solutions to contemporary social problems emphasizing the moral conversion of individuals, in other words, by moralizing. There are other texts that clearly put primary emphasis on the struggle for structural change and then call for an ethical commitment to make this stuggle more effective, more just and more humane. There are also many ambiguous texts, texts that can be read in one way or the other. In my opinion the preaching of Grand'Maison is not always totally free of this ambiguity.

What is the political meaning of Grand'Maison's own preaching? Unsympathetic readers have looked upon him as an old-fashioned clerical preacher, still seeing Quebec as an organic society, still promoting the corporatist ideal, still discouraging political and social struggles because people are not yet virtuous enough.[15] I think these critics are quite wrong.

The vehemence of Grand'Maison's ethical preaching comes from an important insight based on experience, one that is curiously absent among most activists and political scientists, be they liberal, social democratic, or socialist. The insight is that even the most perfect social institution works well only if people are personally dedicated to its aims and purpose. Institutions do not function well without an appropriate ethic. Thus the best health system works well and serves the community only if the participants — doctors, hospital managers, nurses, and patients — are committed to an appropriate ethic, the staff to an ethic of service and the clients to a corresponding modesty, an unwillingness to burden the system excessively. No institution is able to fulfil its aim and purpose without an often renewed moral commitment by all actors. Grand'Maison believes, moreover, that if ethical commitment is to be widespread, it must be mediated and rehearsed through an appropriate culture!

This insight into the role of ethics has been overlooked by political thinkers of the right and the left, even though it is verified by daily experience. On the right, a mechanistic, technocratic understanding of society has persuaded people that social mechanisms work according to their scientific logic, independent of human subjectivity. On the left, political thinkers have been so convinced that human consciousness is shaped by the economic infrastructure that they have supposed that egalitarian social and economic institutions would generate the appropriate attitudes and values almost automatically.

It is significant that the current critical literature, responding to the crisis of Marxist socialism, is attempting to recover the cultural and ethical dimension of the struggle for economic justice. In this context Grand'Maison's insistence on ethical commitment, reiterated by him over the last two decades, appears ahead of his time.

Grand'Maison has also been ahead of his time in recognizing the need for what he has called "communitarian counter-structures."[16] Since the dominant structures — political, economic, educational or trade unionist — do not permit citizen participation and thus alienate the population, people should use their freedom to set up smaller communitarian structures that allow participation and empower their members. These smaller groupings should not become parallel structures meant to replace the dominant structures eventually. Such an aim Grand'Maison would regard as utopian and illusory. The smaller groups, he has argued, should become communitarian counter-structures that provide a caring milieu for their members, offer a practical critique of the cultural mainstream and at certain moments generate the power to transform the dominant structures. In Grand'Maison's books this recommendation does not remain an abstract formula: on the contrary, he has described in detail what certain communitarian counter-structures have achieved and has explained the ways these groupings from different spheres have organized their co-operative efforts. In Grand'Maison's writing is the conviction that neither capitalism nor socialism in any of their forms has been capable of resolving today's economic, societal and cultural problems. He believes that something is being born today beyond capitalism and socialism: a participatory society building itself from below through local initiatives, co-operatives, worker-owned and community-owned economic institutions, citizens' groups, neighbourhood associations, and self-help groups of various kinds. According to Grand'Maison, this is taking place at the margins of society in the popular sectors. It is occurring not among the powerful, the transnationals, big business, big government or even the big labour unions, but among the ordinary people who are discovering their social power. While Grand'Maison refuses to formulate his hopes for society as an ideology, a reading of his books gives the impression that his vision of society has a certain affinity with what is sometimes called *un socialisme cogestionnaire*, a decentralized form of socialism that has integrated the values and institutions of the co-operative movement.

Chapter Five

Douglas Hall: Contextual Theology

Douglas Hall, ordained minister in the United Church of Canada and professor at McGill University, is a distinguished Protestant theologian whose books and articles have been taken very seriously and exercised considerable influence in the Protestant churches of English Canada and the United States. His 1989 publication, *Thinking the Faith*, is the first volume of a projected trilogy, a three-volume systematic theology.[1]

In his theology Douglas Hall wants to reply to the pastoral question: what does the Gospel mean or what should it mean to contemporary Christians living in the culture of North America? In this endeavour he elucidates the response of the Gospel to the predicament of Canadian society. A Montreal resident, Hall is also sensitive to the effort of Quebecers to define their social and political reality. As we shall see, this Canadian theologian also has a message for Quebec.

Despite his interest in culture and public consciousness, Hall remains essentially a theologian. His books and articles are addressed to Christians in search of guidance and understanding. In this respect his writings differ considerably from the work of the Quebec theologian Jacques Grand'Maison, who is engaged in a dialogue with political and social science and for the most part addresses his books and articles to concerned Quebecers, whether they be Catholic or secular.

Douglas Hall is a Protestant theologian whose reading of Christian thought and history differs, not surprisingly, from the interpretations offered in the Catholic tradition. For instance, Hall is greatly impressed by the diversity of teaching and lack of consensus in the Christian church from the apostolic age forward, while Catholics tend to put more emphasis on the creeds and other institutional elements that express the essential unity and coherence of the internally diversified church.

It is not my intention to explore confessional differences in this chapter. It would in fact be possible to show that as a Protestant thinker greatly influenced by Martin Luther's *theologia crucis*, Hall affirms many aspects of the theological enterprise that make him an heir of the Catholic tradition. He takes with utmost seriousness our common heritage, the Christian tradition; he offers an interpretation of *sola scriptura* that rejects biblicism in any of its forms and is critical of theologians who jump from the apostolic age right to the present. Hall has, moreover, a strong communal and ecclesial sense. Since faith takes place in community, theology itself must be carried on in a community of Christians in critical conversation with one another and the church as a whole. Theology exercises therefore an ecclesial responsibility: it is distorted if it becomes the research projects of individual scholars to be evaluated exclusively in terms of the academy.

Contextual theology

The important contribution for which Hall is well-known is his concept of contextual theology. His work is an undisguised attack on the kind of theology that he believes is usually taught at divinity schools and theological faculties. What is wrong with the dominant theology is that it claims to be universal, true and meaningful everywhere, transcending its own historical context. In classical theology this transcendence was located in the universality of truth. Ideas were believed to escape the contingency of the empirical world. Truth, including Christian truth, was seen as objective, universally valid and applicable to all particular situations, whatever the circumstances. Even in modern theology when greater attention was paid to the believing subject, to his or her experiences, theology continued to claim universality because the human condition — interpreted with the help of phenomenology, existentialism or psychology — was believed to be the same everywhere. Since the human predicament was held to be universal, so was the redemptive wisdom derived from the Gospel.

Hall refutes this claim to universality. He argues that European theology, whether Catholic or Protestant, classical or modern, thought of itself as universal and imposed itself on the churches of North America and other continents. Christians in the colonies were taught to look to the European churches as the source of all wisdom. Traditional theology, he argues, did not recognize how embedded in a particular culture it actually was and how much it reflected the social conditions under which it was created. In these circumstances the claim to universality actually played an ideological role legitimating the centrality of Europe in the political history of the world.

Hall insists that the great theological thinkers — Paul, Augustine, Luther, Kierkegaard and many others — reflected on the Gospel from a perspective defined by the conditions of their lives. Hence their theology provided a response to their dilemmas and the dilemmas of their contemporaries. Christian existence is always rooted, Hall argues. Because faith is embedded in life, theology, the intelligent exploration of faith, must deal with the concrete, historical conditions of people's lives.

Such an approach, Hall realizes, gives rise to what is sometimes called the "indigenization" or "enculturation" of the Christian message. Such an intellectual effort is not without danger: it might encourage Christians to follow the spirit of the culture and adapt the Gospel to the needs of their society. To avoid this false understanding of contextual theology Hall appeals to the principle, called after Luther *theologia crucis*, that plays an important role in his entire theological work. In this respect, *theologia crucis* demands that the Christian take a critical look at the dominant secular and religious culture, recognize its self-serving and self-flattering elements, and discern its breaking-point, its feet of clay, its sinful and possibly idolatrous dimension. Unless theology sees itself as the heir of what Hall calls "the prophetic tradition" and uncovers the blind spots of the dominant secular and religious culture, it becomes a *theologia gloriae* and ceases to communicate Christ's redemptive message. He therefore defines contextual theology as *theologia crucis*. Its aim is not simply to find an indigenous expression of the Gospel, but to understand the culture of the place in terms of the forces that threaten it, make it unjust and inhuman, and call for rescue and transformation.

Hall's concept of *theologia crucis* merits a more extended treatment than I can give here.[2] My brief observations suggest that his contextual theology has a certain affinity with liberation theology and the Catholic and Protestant theologies influenced by it. The difference — in my judgment — is that the latter theologies defend the contextual character of theology with the help of sociological reflections derived from a critical dialogue with Marxist thought.

I will amplify this last observation. According to liberation theology the dominant ideas that define a culture, including the dominant theology, tend to express the interests of the dominant sector of society and hence act as an ideology defending the existing power relations. The universality of truth affirmed in the classical tradition expressed the tendency of the Mediterranean world to see itself as the normative representative of civilized humanity. It was assumed that beyond its borders lived only barbarians. To the extent that the churches identified themselves with the dominant sector of their societies in the classical period and subsequent ages, their theologies also tended to legitimate the existing order.

In the above sentences I have used the noun "tendency" and the verb "tend" advisedly. Liberation theologians reject Marxist theory which supposes that certain laws capable of being known scientifically are operative in society. These theologians avoid quick generalizations and prefer to speak of trends and tendencies operative in society. They hold, therefore, that in each concrete situation examination is needed to discover to what extent the churches and their theologies have become reflections of the establishment and the dominant culture. Even when churches bless the existing order, theology is often full of surprises.

With Hall liberation theology argues, against existentialism and much of modern theology, that the human predicament is not universal. To suppose that the human predicament is identical for all people whatever their social location — for the colonizers and the colonized, for the rich and the poor, for the defenders of apartheid and the people it marginalizes — is to trivialize the situation of the victims and thus to render invisible the injustices that cry to high heaven.

Let us return to Douglas Hall. The Canadian theologian fully recognizes the difficulties raised by contextual theology (and liberation theology) and offers carefully thought-out replies to these difficulties.[3] I will briefly mention two of them: (1) while the Gospel of Jesus presents itself as a universal message addressed to people everywhere, contextual theology appears to focus on a certain region and thus limit the scope of the divine message; (2) while Jesus remains the same yesterday, today and tomorrow, contextual theology appears to undermine the self-identity of the Christian message throughout time.

To the first difficulty Hall replies that we cannot come to a true understanding of our own situation unless we locate it in the wider context and relate it to what is taking place on the global level. Contextual theology, therefore, takes into account the entire world situation, but looks upon it from a particular perspective. Since contextual theology is a *theologia crucis*, it generates solidarity with the victims of society everywhere and the prophetic voices that reveal the ambiguity of the dominant culture. Contextual theology is therefore not parochial but in its own way reaches out for universality. Liberation theology makes the same claim, except that the argument it offers is sociologically more precise. Liberation theology demands that theology, in whatever society it is developed should be "holistic," i.e. it should include among its concerns the relationship of the society to the rest of the world. To do this it is necessary to analyze the bonds of political and economic power, whether of domination or dependency, that relate a society to the world. Thus Latin American liberation theologians remind theologians in the United States that they, the Americans, cannot come to a correct understanding of their society unless they think holistically by recognizing the imperialistic relations of the United States to the poor countries of the south.

Thanks to his *theologia crucis* Hall has an intuitive sense that the self-perception of the developed societies is distorted if it disregards their relationships to the Third World.

What about the second difficulty, the self-identity of the Gospel throughout time? Is this identity not undermined by contextual theology? Hall deals with this question at great length. He devises a theological methodology that assures the fidelity of contextual theology to the one Gospel, to the one Jesus, his message and his work. Since the *theologia crucis* is an essential element of this methodology, the self-identity of the Gospel cannot be guaranteed by clinging to the inherited dogmatic affirmations. The sameness of the Gospel reveals itself in its power to uncover the truth about our culture, to offer hope for deliverance from its sins and to generate the newness of life in this predicament. It is therefore precisely the contextuality of theology that assures the abiding, unchanging character of the Christian message.

Liberation theology in the Catholic stream does not give up on dogmatic affirmations quite so quickly. Just as Catholic liberation theologians reread the biblical books, giving priority to the prophetic dimension and thus highlighting the message of liberation, so they also reread the church's dogmatic tradition to uncover its hidden, radical implications. Some theologians, for instance, see in the dogma of the Trinity the rejection of a monarchical concept of divinity that has been used to legitimate monarchical government and one-man regimes in human institutions. In this chapter I can go no further in exploring the difference between Protestant and Catholic approaches. I will leave this all too brief examination of contextual theology and turn to Douglas Hall's analysis of the North American context.

The North American context

The culture of North America belongs to the western world defined by the Enlightenment, industrialization, technological reason and the philosophy of inevitable progress. In the nineteenth century evolution was the key concept that created the cultural optimism of Europeans and North Americans. The liberal Protestant theology of that day sometimes even equated Christianity with the high point of this cultural evolution.

In Europe, Hall argues, the first world war created a painful cultural upheaval.[4] Ever wider circles of critical thinkers came to recognize the problematic nature of scientific rationality and the threat it posed to European civilization. The mood of the people was dark and fearful. In this historical context Karl Barth's dialectical theology brought out the truth and power of the Gospel. The world lay in darkness, he announced: human wisdom was folly, trust in progress was insanity. Truth and life were found in Jesus Christ alone. Hall greatly appreciates the work of Barth. Yet what went wrong, Hall argues, is that Barth's theology, obviously a contextual response to the post-war European experience, came to be regarded by Barthians as universally valid and applicable to historical conditions which it was never meant to address.

In North America the modern faith in progress remained undisturbed. This was true principally in the United States, yet to some extent also in Canada — which so often means English Canada. Cultural optimism constituted the dominant mood. Several uniquely American experiences intensified the success-orientation of American culture: Americans saw themselves as the new world rescued from European decadence, the originating home of egalitarian democracy, the country with an open border moving west, the land of endless opportunities, the vanguard of human evolution and the model for all other societies. While there were important critical voices, secular and religious, in the United States — Hall praises Reinhold Niebuhr as a critic of American society — the faith in social progress and personal success remained intact in American culture including the churches, and especially in the Protestant churches. There were of course great setbacks, painful experiences of depression and wars, but the people believed that once these difficulties were overcome progress would continue its upward climb. People kept their faith in the American system.

Hall proposes the provocative thesis that American-ism and Protestantism have become amalgamated.[5] The prophetic voices in the Protestant churches were never strong enough to shake the foundations of American culture. The classical Reformation, including Calvin's own theology, had a lively sense of sin and hence en-tertained a strong suspicion toward the modern world in the making. Yet later Calvinist piety contained cer-tain elements that made an identification with an opti-mistic, ambitious, upwardly-mobile culture possible. There is in Hall's work an echo of Max Weber's thesis that the Protestant ethos had a certain affinity with the spirit of capitalism. In the United States and some other parts of the world, the Calvinist concept of covenant, inadequately understood, lent itself to legitimate the collective self-understanding of the newly created soci-ety as "God's own country."

This cultural optimism, Hall argues, has today be-come an extreme form of false consciousness. The ob-servable historical trends have actually brought west-ern culture in general and American society in particu-lar to an acute crisis from which they may never re-cover. The Holocaust has revealed the genocidal ca-pacity of the modern state; the nuclear arms race has brought humanity close to self-destruction; the unre-strained production of goods is exhausting the natural resources and devastating the natural environment es-sential for human survival; the development of a global economy is widening the gap between rich and poor, leaving vast third-world populations in conditions of chronic misery and hunger and creating growing pockets of poverty even in the industrialized countries. A nuclear exchange, a major ecological accident or the collapse of the global economy into a world-wide de-pression could happen soon.

The refusal of American society to recognize the truth of the historical situation has destructive cultural consequences. As people repress their fear and insecurity and keep on trusting the rational thrust of modern society, they fall into various patterns of irrational behaviour. Some become vulnerable to mental disturbance; some seek the immediate satisfaction of desire without thought for tomorrow; some cling to the oversimplified answers and securities offered by evangelical sectarianism. The neo-conservative vision of society (called more correctly *néo-libérale* in Québec) is a new, more unbelievable version of the nineteenth-century liberal dream that allowing the clever, the rich and the powerful to promote their economic interests will eventually benefit the whole of society, including the poor. People still seem to believe this message. The resourceful entrepreneur has again become the hero of society. In contrast men and women who have an inkling of the danger in which we live and realize the urgent need for radical change have become a small minority without voice or impact, at odds with mainstream culture.

In this context, Hall argues, the theology of the cross must announce the gospel of failure. Divine revelation promises neither material progress nor personal success but simply faith, hope and love. Christians in the declining American empire must learn to live with failure and find God in it. At this time there are no easy answers, no blueprints for success, no solutions that can be applied. If we search too quickly for a strategy to overcome the present crisis, we still allow ourselves to be guided by faith in progress. Since we remain optimists refusing to acknowledge the data of despair, we will never find the way. What is needed, Hall argues, is entry into the *via negativa*, the recognition of failure, the acknowledgment of having gone astray, the total disillusionment with modernity and its technological rationality.

In this connection Hall makes a few remarks critical of North American practitioners of liberation theology.[6] He believes that the reliance of North American liberation theology on sociological analysis, correct theory and strategies of solidarity is still carried by the Enlightenment hope that modern reason, possibly guided by faith, is the organ of human progress and that the modern project based on rationality can be saved. For Hall this North American liberation theology contains an element of illusion that still has to be surrendered.

It would be wrong to read Douglas Hall as a Karl Barth *revividus*. Hall recognizes — as Barth does not — the power of the gracious God in secular experience. Here the Canadian theologian is closer to Paul Tillich. The negative judgment on modern society, the despair over the common faith in progress and the conversion to human relations that heal, restore and reconcile are mediated not only by those who believe in Christ but also and especially by prophetic voices that speak out of secular experiences. These voices include representatives of the poor and the marginalized; contextual theologians must be in dialogue with them. These prophetic voices also include poets and artists. Douglas Hall likes Marshall McLuhan's famous *bon mot* that the artists are the DEW (Distant Early Warning) line of civilization.[7]

Hall's theological studies constantly refer to poets and novelists, especially Canadian authors, to confirm and illustrate the theological proposals under discussion. With Paul Tillich, he believes that God's ever gracious power stirring up new life and new opportunities in unexpected ways is present in the constellation of evil which surrounds us. The gospel of failure, which the American churches must preach today, is not a call to otherworldliness nor is it simply a message of gloom and doom for earthly life. Responding to the present ecological upheaval, Hall even calls for a needed conversion to the earth in his theology of divine creation and human stewardship. It is true, of course, that the gospel of failure makes us sad and summons us to mourn over the useless suffering our society inflicts on vast numbers of people.

But this gospel remains good news. For in this crisis situation God does not leave us without consolation, vision, and hope.

Where do we encounter God's redemptive presence? In unexpected places. In the words of some simple and some sophisticated people and in the commitment of Christians and non-Christians to alternative social projects, we learn that God is alive and at work among us, preparing a new day. It is the task of contextual theology to be close to these redemptive events, to remember them, to tell their story, and to foster the quiet hope that God at work among people is laying a new foundation. But what this foundation is precisely, and what social project it calls for, and what we should be doing at the present time; these things are not yet clear. We are not to jump on these redemptive experiences as the new recipe for success; we are rather to wait patiently and impatiently until the entire culture has abandoned the illusion of progress.

This, Hall believes, is the Christian perception of the North American context. How are we to unfold the Christian story in this historical situation? How in this context do we present the Christian creed, the doctrines of God, Jesus and the divine Spirit sent into the world? Douglas Hall will reply to these questions in the second volume of his trilogy. Yet we find many hints and the outline of his thought already in his published work.

The Canadian context

What matters here is Hall's understanding of the Canadian situation. When he speaks of the North American context, he means primarily the United States even though he also includes the Dominion of Canada. Is such an approach fully justified? This is a genuine problem experienced by critical thinkers in countries with a relatively small population.

Gustavo Gutierrez does not write his theology for Peru, the country where he belongs, nor does the Brazilian Leonardo Boff write his books simply for the Brazilian church. What Latin American authors produce is a contextual theology for the whole of Latin America. They do this in part because the countries on that continent have much in common — a common colonial history, a common cultural heritage (Iberian culture imposed on the original population), a common Catholic tradition and a common experience of dependency on foreign powers — even though there are also significant differences among them. Another motive for authors from different countries to produce a Latin American liberation theology is their desire to promote a greater sense of solidarity among Latin American nations, whose populations are often caught in competitive nationalisms that inhibit them from discovering the true causes of their poverty and powerlessness. There may also be a very practical reason why these authors produce their theology for the entire Latin American continent: they need a wider readership than the one available in their own country. How else can they find a publisher for their books? How else can they join the conversation taking place on the entire continent?

Anglophone Canadian authors have a similar problem. If they deal with a specifically Canadian topic, they try to publish their manuscripts in Canada, realizing that they will not be read in the United States and thus not join the pertinent conversation going on in that vast country. If, on the other hand, anglophone Canadian authors deal with more general issues in literature, history, social science, theology, or other fields — issues in other words that transcend the specifically Canadian debate — then they prefer to address themselves to the vaster anglophone community and publish their books in Great Britain or now more often in the United States.

When Hall writes on specifically Canadian issues, he publishes his books in Canada. Yet when he addresses the theological problems that challenge the churches imprisoned in the optimistic, success-oriented culture of industrial, capitalist North America, he writes books that speak to a wider North American audience. His books may from time to time mention the similar and yet slightly different Canadian situation, but they confine the Canadian material to a minimum. Otherwise he would not find an American publisher, and the Canadian theologian would not be able to join the important theological debate in the United States.

For Hall this is a dilemma. He does not want to promote what anglophone Canadians call "continentalism," the policy that favours the integration of the Canadian economy into the larger, more developed economy of the United States. On the contrary, he is a Canadian nationalist. Together with the labour unions, more than one political party, progressive intellectuals and the Christian churches, Douglas Hall vehemently opposed the fateful free-trade agreement between Canada and the United States. At the same time, he believes that the optimistic, success-oriented American culture has so powerfully invaded Canadian society that today North Americans, be they Canadians or Americans, suffer from the same cultural disease. North American Christians on both sides of the border are equally blind to the profound crisis that threatens world society. They use the gospel of Jesus to feel good, become cheery and be reconciled to the present system: they thus aggravate the illness of society. The gospel of failure, Hall argues, is relevant in the United States and in Canada.

In his small 1980 book, *The Canada Crisis*, published in Canada, he presents his reflections on the specifically Canadian context in greater detail. Here Hall reveals how much he is influenced by the critical ideas of the Canadian philosopher, George Grant, even though the theologian does not follow Grant into his philosophy.

Grant's brilliant little book, *Lament for a Nation*,[8] published in 1965 after the defeat of John Diefenbaker, tried to demonstrate that Canadian society had ceased to exist as a country defined by its own history and its own culture. According to Grant, most Canadians, including the so-called progressive intellectuals and politicians, were unaware of "this defeat of Canadian nationalism." When, as prime minister, Diefenbaker adopted foreign and domestic policies against the wishes of the United States and Canadian business interests, he was rejected by the majority of Canadians, including the Canadian left, because people had lost the sense that they constituted a nation.

Even if the reader disagrees with this particular analysis, Grant provides ample evidence for his thesis that in the past Canadians had a sense of their own cultural identity as being both British and North American and including a distinct people, the French Canadians. This cultural identity, which embraced the values of community, order, modesty, and closeness to nature, was as yet untouched by the dream of becoming bigger and better. Grant believed that the aggressive American culture, an extreme form of utilitarian rationality recently oriented toward technological empire, had successfully invaded Canadian society, undermined the Canadian cultural identity, and transformed Canada into a satellite nation, a watered-down version of the United States.

Hall is in basic agreement with Grant's famous thesis. In *The Canada Crisis* Hall uses two poetic images to illustrate the temptation of Canadians to imitate American society and the vocation of Canadians to define their own society in independent terms. Canadians are tempted by "the Florida sun": by the culture of youth, pleasure and success, by the mood of optimism that looks forward to never-ending material progress and expects ingenious technical solutions to solve the problems of society. By contrast, the prophetic message summons Canadians living in the north to treasure their "winter light": their tradition of measure and modesty that preserves the human dimension in social, political and economic life. Canadians are free to choose between "Florida sun" and "winter light" only if they are conscious of their own history. But, alas, most Canadians have lost their memory. They refuse to remember. The country and the majority of its citizens, according to Hall's analysis, have assimilated the watered-down version of the American dream. In this situation, the Christian message is clear. According to the *theologia crucis*, it is only in "winter light" that the divine promises find earthly fulfilment.

Where does Hall find the moments of grace in Canadian society? His theology of the cross does not ask Christians to turn their back on the world and look for fulfilment in a higher, spiritual order. Contextual theology demands that Christians take the world with new seriousness. In the midst of the crisis, underneath the dominant trends, prophetic voices and healing events continue to be present — because God is gracious. Where does Hall find these voices and these events in Canada? He mentions Canadian poets, novelists and painters; he mentions the Canadian tradition of co-operation in co-operatives and labour unions. He refers to the political inheritance of the Co-operative Commonwealth Federation (CCF). He also mentions Quebec's Quiet Revolution.[9]

Why Quebec? Hall admires Quebec because it had not surrendered to any version of the American dream. He wrote this in 1980! Quebec had lived in "winter light." He interpreted the awakening of Quebec in the Quiet Revolution not as a frantic effort to catch up with modern North American society but, on the contrary, as an imaginative effort to build an alternative North American society still based on communal values, on solidarity, mutuality, social democracy and modest wishes for material well-being. Hall loves the slogan, "Je me souviens." Quebecers still want to remember. When the Parti Québécois came to power in 1976, Hall believed that, despite certain worrisome elements in the party platform, something exciting and hopeful was taking place in Quebec. Out of suffering and memory Quebecers were building a society that would transcend the individualism and materialism characteristic of English-speaking North America. It is not my intention to examine the validity of his evaluation of the Quiet Revolution. Historians of this revolution have given much prominence to the process of modernization and hence to *rattrapage* or catching-up present in this great upheaval of Quebec society. Douglas Hall is especially sensitive to the other side, the cultural dimension and the emphasis on solidarity and social democracy.

A resident of Montreal's English section, he was greatly saddened by the totally negative reaction of English Montrealers to the victory of the Parti Québécois. He wanted anglophone Canadians to learn from Quebec nationalism, remember their own past, stop imitating the Americans, recognize their "winter light" situation and create an independent Canada with its own cultural identity. He grieved particularly that anglophone Christians simply repeated the prejudices of secular interpreters and refused to look at Quebec events from a theological point of view.

As a member of the United Church Committee on French-English Relations, Douglas Hall was asked to prepare a statement to be submitted to the entire Montreal Presbytery, a declaration that would articulate an anglophone Christian perspective on Quebec developments. The declaration was approved by the committee, but got mired in the legal procedures bringing it to the presbytery. Still the statement, eventually called the Montreal Declaration, was published in a number of reviews.[10] It appears at the end of this chapter.

Remaining ambiguity

There is a certain ambiguity in Hall's contextual theology that makes it difficult to evaluate it fully. What is his perception of the western Enlightenment tradition? He certainly rejects the naive and uncritical affirmation of modern rationality implicit in the dominant western culture, especially in North America. The reliance on technological reason as the guide to truth and freedom is for him the principal cause for the contemporary crisis. But does he follow philosophers such as George Grant who think that the Enlightenment was simply a tragic mistake? Was the Enlightenment trust that "reason" could become the organ of human self-emancipation an expression of Promethean hubris that paved the way for the great disasters of modernity? Or is Hall's evaluation of the Enlightenment more subtle? Does he, after his passionate critique of technological rationality, still attempt to retrieve certain elements of the Enlightenment?

This is an issue with important practical consequences. Do all technological developments tend to transform humans into objects and hence dehumanize society in the long run, or is it possible to devise a critique of technology that would enable society, if it so chose, to invent technologies that serve its humanization? Or, should one remain aloof from the struggles of societal victims for emancipation because, in their attempts to transform the present order, they still rely on the liberating power of reason? Or is it possible to define conditions for supporting emancipatory movements?

It is my opinion that with regard to this important issue Hall's contextual theology remains undecided. On the one hand, there are brief passages, already mentioned, where he is critical of North American liberation theology because it still clings to the illusion that the modern project can be saved. It proposes, in other words, that there is an emancipatory rationality that could and should guide the struggle for the reconstruction of society. On the other hand, Hall refuses to join George Grant in the return to pre-modern, classical philosophy. In fact Hall's affirmation of contextuality and rejection of the classical notion that truth is universal emerge from a modern, historical approach to truth derived from the Enlightenment tradition. He quotes with approval Bernard Lonergan's distinction between the classicist and the modern approach to thought, culture and theology.[11] Because theology is modern, Hall argues, it must be in critical dialogue with its culture, including social and political science. Hall seems to both negate and affirm modern rationality.

This chapter is not the vehicle to discuss in detail the questions raised by this ambiguity. It is my impression that when Anglo-American thinkers speak of the Enlightenment, they have in mind primarily the British empiricist tradition, particularly John Locke and later the Utilitarians: their rejection of metaphysics, the indifference to virtue, the sole reliance on enlightened self-interest and eventually the surrender to scientific positivism and technological rationality.

By contrast, when German thinkers mention the Enlightenment they tend to think of Immanuel Kant. They recognize that Enlightenment rationality had two dimensions, one empirical and scientific and the other ethical and emancipatory. When French thinkers mention the Enlightenment, they include Jean-Jacques Rousseau, the great philosopher whose notion of emancipatory reason included communal, ethical and symbolic concerns neglected by earlier Enlightenment thinkers. The philosophical movement of the Enlightenment had several dimensions.

In the twenties of this century a group of philosophers, founders of the Frankfurt School — with whom the theologian Paul Tillich was closely associated — wrestled with the question later raised by George Grant and Douglas Hall. The Frankfurters recognized that in the present the Enlightenment had become an obstacle to the humanization of life. Enlightenment rationality had collapsed into scientific positivism and technological reason. Reason had become purely instrumental. A society guided by instrumental reason, they argued, would inevitably instrumentalize and thus dehumanize the human beings who belonged to it. For the Frankfurt School, unlimited progress through technological rationality was the dangerous myth that put modern society on a train racing through the night toward certain destruction.

What should our reaction be to this state of affairs? Should we regard the Enlightenment as a terrible mistake, as a historical project inspired by control, mastery and domination? Should we return to pre-Enlightenment sources of wisdom? To Aristotle — as did the Thomists? To Plato — as did Simone Weil and George Grant? Or possibly to the pre-Socratic philosophers — as did Martin Heidegger? Or should we return with the Romantics to greater reliance on traditional values, the inherited sense of community and the feelings generated by religious, ethnic or racial solidarity?

The philosophers of the Frankfurt School, including Paul Tillich, said "no" to these responses. They believed it was ultimately dangerous to abandon the emancipatory commitment of the Enlightenment altogether. Why? Because all the great philosophical, religious and cultural traditions contained elements of domination damaging to certain sectors of society — to women or to certain classes or races. These dominating elements need the critique of ethical, emancipatory reason. For the Frankfurt philosophers the Enlightenment was much richer than the scientific positivism and instrumental rationality that had come to prevail in contemporary society. Relying on Rousseau, Kant, and subsequent emancipatory thinkers, these philosophers argued that Enlightenment rationality embraced two dimensions, one empirical-scientific and the other ethical-humanistic. Together they constituted reason as the organ of human self-emancipation.

It was later, in the second half of the nineteenth century — in Germany this was the beginning of industrialization — that the collapse of reason into scientific-technological rationality occurred. Since then, the Frankfurters argued, the Enlightenment has become the great obstacle to the humanization of society. What are we to do? For the reasons mentioned, it would be dangerous to negate the entire modern project. What is required, these philosophers argued, is that we "negate" the primacy assigned to technological reason and then, after exploring the full implications of this negation, "retrieve" the ethical dimension of the original Enlightenment project.

An example of such a "negation" and "retrieval" would be the post-second world war affirmation of human rights. The negation: human beings are not means, instruments or objects, even though they are seen as such by technological reason and treated as such by technological society. The retrieval: in the light of the emancipatory reason of the Enlightenment, which is still part of our heritage, human beings have a transcendent dignity as subjects, as agents responsible for their world.

The Frankfurt philosophers called this process of negation and retrieval "the dialectical negation" of the Enlightenment. They strongly opposed any non-dialectical negation of the Enlightenment because they feared that such steps would foster indifference to inequality and oppression and ultimately generate structures at odds with human rights. Paul Tillich, both in his early, socialist phase in Germany and in his later, cultural phase in the United States, practised the dialectical negation of Enlightenment reason. I can find traces of this dialectic in the theological work of Douglas Hall himself. Thus he recommends that contextual theologians be in dialogue with modern thinkers who retrieve reflective forms of reason beyond instrumental rationality.[12] Yet according to my reading of his work,

Hall never makes it perfectly clear if together with the Canadian George Grant, the French theologian Jacques Ellul and the American theologian Gibson Winter he opts for a non-dialectical negation of the Enlightenment. Or does he follow his great teacher, Paul Tillich, into a dialectical negation — the negation, incidentally, also practised by liberation theology. The consequences of this choice for social ethics and political solidarity are considerable.

APPENDIX TO CHAPTER FIVE

A Montreal Declaration

We, the representatives of the Montreal Presbytery of the United Church of Canada, conscious of the opportunities for Christian work and witness opening to us at this time, wish to clarify our intention under God to serve him and our fellow citizens of Quebec and Canada faithfully and with imagination. Addressing ourselves in particular to the anglophone community of Quebec, and to the United Church of Canada. . . .

1. We affirm that the Spirit of the God who acted decisively in Jesus our Lord for the liberation of mankind is ever at work in the world "to make and to keep human life human."

We lament, therefore, every form of cynicism which sees in political and other events in history nothing but the will of man and the clash of power with power.

2. We affirm that while no human deed, achievement or program should ever be identified unqualifiedly with the will of God, historical events which offer humanity a way into the future are never without a transcendent dimension.

We lament, for this reason, the tendency of some within the Christian churches to place God's providence so far above the historical flux as effectively to deny his love for the world.

3. We affirm the new sense of hope that has come to inspire our francophone fellow citizens at this time; we give thanks for their openness to the future, and want to share in their enthusiasm for new possibilities of human community in this place.

We lament, therefore, the tendency of some of our anglophone brothers and sisters to give way to feelings of personal anxiety, resentment, and cultivated apathy, so that they miss the awareness of opportunities implicit in our present situation.

4.   We affirm that Christians are called to involve themselves in the affairs of human communities, and without pride or quest for power to assume responsibility for society.

Thus we lament the retreat of many anglophones from this province, and the abdication of responsibility on the part of many who remain.

5.   We affirm the manifest need for an anglophone community in Quebec — "a new breed of anglophone" — which is committed to the good destiny of this province and its unique contribution to Canada.

We lament, therefore, the continuing spirit of narrowly racial, economic and other interests, which gives priority to self-preservation and to the fostering of ends which deny Christ's call to human solidarity.

6.   We affirm that we are prepared to live in Quebec as part of a minority; we intend to be a creative element within that minority, to support the vision of a better society as it inspires many of our leaders, and to be vigilant for human dignity according to our Christian understanding of the nature of humanity.

We lament for this reason any remnant of false pride which may still keep us and our English-speaking compatriots from accepting the posture of such a minority, wishing instead to play a dominating role.

7.   We affirm that, in view of the grave dangers of a monolithic technocratic society present on this continent, it is essential for concerned Canadians actively to preserve the French language, culture and heritage; and we recognize that in the face of such dangers government may need to resort to what may seem strong or artificial measures in order to achieve this goal.

Hence we lament the failure on the part of many anglophones in Quebec and Canada to manifest a sympathetic comprehension of such measures, on the assumption that the preservation of the French heritage will occur as a matter of course.

8. We affirm that the present conflict is complex and multidimensional; it is not simply a struggle for the maintenance of French Canada but for our country as a distinct entity on this continent and a creative force in world affairs.

Therefore we lament the tendency of some simplistically to construe this as a struggle between French and English elements, and so to miss the larger issues.

9. Finally we affirm that the Church of Jesus Christ transcends racial, national, linguistic and other particularities; yet it is not indifferent to these, for it recognizes that human liberation is always being worked out in the specifics of daily existence.

So we lament, on the one hand, the failure of some Christians to rise above cultural and traditional loyalties to the higher loyalty of faith in the universal Lord, and, on the other hand, the assumption of some that Christian faith ought simply to ignore the particularities of nation, race, speech and culture.

In the confidence that we are not alone, that our God is present in these crises and uncertainties, and that many human beings of good will everywhere can identify themselves with the directions suggested in this Declaration, we commend it to all who care about our land, and especially to the household of faith.

Chapter Six

Ethical Reflections on the Quebec Language Debate

Because I teach social ethics at Montreal's McGill University, I am often asked to comment on the language debate in Quebec society. This complex issue warrants a careful analysis. In this chapter I will clarify the ethical issues involved in the discussion. I work from the assumption that all participants are in good faith. While I will not hide my own position, it is my intention in this chapter to explain how people of good will come to such divergent conclusions. We note that the present debate goes on not only in Quebec; it also proceeds within the Christian churches and the federal political parties.

The facts of the case

First I will look at the historical context. The self-affirmation of French Quebecers in the Quiet Revolution (beginning in 1960) has created a new Quebec where the French-speaking majority plays the dominant role. This development led to several language bills, culminating in the Parti Québécois government's 1977 Bill 101 which made French the public language and the working language of the province. English-speaking Quebecers retained their "historical rights" to English-language institutions: schools, universities, hospitals and social service agencies all in English. But public signs were to be in French only. Companies with more than fifty employees were obliged to carry on their work in French.

French Quebecers looked upon Bill 101 as the charter of the French language that would give them a certain security against the assimilating power of the English language in North America. Bill 101 was the public signal to immigrants and newcomers that their participation in Quebec society would be in French. Many Quebecers regarded Bill 101 as a legal charter beyond political partisanship. The Catholic bishops of Quebec thought that Bill 101 was an historical event that called for a pastoral letter.[1] The Quebec New Democratic Party, despite the federal party's disapproval, stood behind Bill 101's sign law and defended it even after the Supreme Court decision against it.

English-speaking Quebecers were unhappy with Bill 101. Their main complaint was that public signs, including all commercial signs, were to be in French only. Some believed that this rule violated their human rights, in particular their freedom of expression. In the 1985 election campaign Robert Bourassa promised English-speaking Quebecers that his Liberal Party, once in power, would permit bilingual signs. Yet when he became premier, he hesitated. Realizing the enormous popularity of Bill 101, he refused to touch the public sign rule.

Certain anglophone Montrealers took the matter to the courts. On December 15, 1988 the Supreme Court of Canada decided that it was indeed the task of the Quebec government to promote and protect the French language, but that the means employed in this endeavour had to conform to the charter of rights. The Court decided that the rule demanding commercial signs in French only violated people's freedom of expression.

The Bourassa government was in a bind. The great majority of Quebecers, including many Liberal members in the National Assembly, supported Bill 101 as a charter that should not be touched, while the English-speaking population demanded that justice be done as defined by the Supreme Court. Mr. Bourassa sought a compromise solution. He introduced a new law, Bill 178, that endorsed most of the articles of Bill 101 except the sign rule. Bill 178 allowed bilingual commercial signs inside the stores, but continued the requirement for unilingual French signs outside. To make Bill 178 legal he invoked the notwithstanding clause of the Canadian Constitution (which Quebec has not yet signed) to limit the application of the Supreme Court's decision. Newspaper coverage gave the impression that the majority of francophones and the majority of anglophones were unhappy with Bill 178.

Human rights

I will now look at the great ethical tradition solemnly endorsed by the United Nations Universal Declaration of Human Rights of 1948.[2] This tradition has also been recognized by the Christian churches as in keeping with biblical teaching. What is sometimes overlooked is that the human rights tradition has its own complexity. There are personal rights that guarantee civil liberties: the freedoms of expression, of religion, of peaceful assembly and of organization. These rights were fought for, from the seventeenth century forward, against the *ancien régime,* the aristocratic rule that wanted to protect law and order by suppressing people's freedom to speak and to act in public.

Secondly, there are collective rights that entitle peoples to cultural and political self-determination. These rights were claimed by peoples under imperial rule, for instance, in the nineteenth century by the Irish under the British Crown and the Polish under Tsarist Empire. In the twentieth century peoples struggling against political and economic colonial domination have demanded them. Peoples have the right to give themselves governments that protect and promote their values and their culture and the common good. These rights ratified by the United Nations have served as a basis for founding the state of Israel and many other states in Asia and Africa. These rights are not enshrined in a book of law, but they justify in universally-accepted ethical terms political struggles for self-determination and government actions to protect and promote the common good.

Thirdly, there are solidarity rights upholding the just claims of the weak against the power of the strong. These rights include, for instance, the right to eat, the right to shelter, the right to work and the right to form labour organizations. Christians believe that these rights have a special affinity with the scriptures. Here is a sentence drawn from a pastoral of the Canadian Catholic bishops, later endorsed by John Paul II on his visit to Canada: "The needs of the poor have priority over the wants of the rich; the rights of workers are more important than the maximization of profits; the participation of the marginalized groups has precedence over a system that excludes them."[3]

Human rights, because of their complex structure, are often competing with one another. The Quebec language debate emerges from a conflict between collective rights and personal rights. French Quebecers regard Bill 101 as an expression of their collective human right to define their own cultural and social identity, but many anglophones and other communities that speak English in public believe that Bill 101 deprives them of certain personal human rights. Which human right has the priority here? Lawyers and courts tend to look upon this and similar questions from a purely legal perspective. They try to resolve such questions in terms of the existing legislation. But human rights are first of all an ethical reality; they are moral claims. Questions posed by competing human rights therefore call for ethical reflection. Christians in particular will want to deal with these questions in terms of the social ethics belonging to their religious tradition.

Human rights, I will insist, are not absolutes. They are always historically situated. Human rights, moreover, remain ambiguous. In a sinful world they can easily be abused. Collective rights have been invoked by governments to suppress civil liberties. In the name of serving the public good or defending national security, governments have introduced repressive legislation. In Canada, for example, the War Measures Act allowed the government during World War II to intern and dispossess without trial Canadian citizens of Japanese origin. Another example is pre-Vatican II Catholic social teaching, which held that governments of Catholic countries had the moral right to protect the common good, including the established religion, by suppressing the religious freedom of Protestant minorities. In Quebec during the nineteen fifties, this principle was invoked by the Maurice Duplessis government against the Jehovah's Witnesses.

It is also true that personal human rights or civil liberties are ambiguous. They can become part of a political strategy to undermine existing structures of solidarity and promote the individualistic free-enterprise mentality. Emphasis on civil liberties easily creates the illusion that the members of society are all equal and thus disguises the structures of economic inequality. On the basis of these civil rights, individual workers can take a labour union to court for giving financial support to the New Democratic Party (N.D.P.) without the approval of every member or even for violating the freedom of individual workers by imposing a closed-shop rule. Commercial companies can take the government to court for violating freedom of expression when it forbids advertising directed at children under thirteen or when it prohibits the advertising of cigarettes.

What follows from this is that from an ethical point of view the application of human rights, whether collective or personal, is never something unconditional: it always demands an ethical, rational justification. Similarly, conflicts between competing sets of rights must be resolved by ethical, rational arguments.

Is Quebec a nation?

In the case of the Quebec language debate we have to make certain historical judgments that have far-reaching ethical implications. The first question is: are Quebecers a people? Or are they simply French-speaking Canadians, an important minority in the country? We are often confronted with such historical questions. Are the Palestinians a people? Or are they simply groups of Arabs located in the area formerly called Palestine? Are the Estonians a people or simply an ethnic group strongly represented in one of the republics in the Soviet Union? The answers to such questions have ethical consequences. A people has the human right to self-determination; it is entitled to define its own cultural and political identity. According to the 1966 International Covenant on Civil and Political Rights of the United Nations, "All peoples have the right to self-determination: by virtue of this right they freely determine their political status and freely pursue their economic, social and cultural development."[4]

Another way of posing the question about Quebec is to ask whether Canada is a nation state like France, a binational state like Belgium, or a multi-national state like Yugoslavia? When we answer this question we must be careful not to forget the Native peoples who have lived here from time immemorial. It is not unfair to say that until recently, most English-speaking Canadians regarded Canada as a nation state — a state including a single nation — and considered French-Canadians an important and honoured ethnic minority, one of the founding groups of this country. Quebec was considered simply as one of the ten provinces.

Only in the sixties, responding to the noise of the Quiet Revolution, the federal political parties, especially the Progressive Conservatives and the N.D.P., began to recognize the peoplehood of French Canadians and to advocate a special status for Quebec within Confederation. It was also during the sixties that the Canadian Catholic church acknowledged the Quebec community as a people.[5]

Are there norms that specify with some precision what peoplehood means? Usually peoplehood is defined with reference to a set of objective and subjective factors. The objective factors include a definable territory, common language, common culture, common history and the existence of political and economic institutions that bind people together and render them capable of acting in concert. The subjective factor is the collective will to constitute a people. This political will is usually generated by special historical experiences. Thus the Jews began to think of themselves as a nation in the political sense mainly as a response to the persecutions and later the genocide inflicted on them. The Palestinians developed a strong sense of peoplehood as a response to the powers that made them second-class citizens in their own land.

If this is a valid definition, it is difficult to deny that Quebecers constitute a people. Both the objective and subjective factors seem to be present. French Quebecers think of themselves as a people, even when they are convinced federalists and oppose the independence movement.

This conclusion has been challenged by an important argument. Pierre Elliot Trudeau has defended the view that French Canadians spread over the whole of Canada, not Quebecers, constitute a people. If this were true, then peoplehood would have a much weaker meaning. This sort of peoplehood would not ground the right to self-determination since French Canadians hold no common territory and have no political and economic institutions that enable them to act collectively.

An answer to this argument is that historical forces have so weakened the country-wide presence of French Canadians that there remains only one core territory, Quebec, where French Canadians constitute the majority and where the government protects the language and promotes the cultural institutions, such as colleges, universities, research institutes and publishing houses, that are indispensable for a modern, developed society.

A colonized people

The next historical question we will examine is more controversial. The answer has important ethical implications. Is the self-empowerment of Quebecers in the Quiet Revolution part of a longer struggle against colonial subjugation starting with the British conquest? Were Quebecers an oppressed people? In other words, is the new Quebec with the dominant French presence in public life, industry, commerce, and culture — including Bills 101 and 178 — the righting of a previous wrong? Is it, in part at least, redress of a colonial situation? Was the Quiet Revolution the outcome of a collective struggle against the economic, cultural and linguistic hegemony exercised by the anglophone elite in the province?

Most French Quebecers believe that this is so. In particular, members of the older generation who remember the inherited patterns of social inequality are keenly aware of the colonization inflicted upon their people in the past. They are able to muster strong, rational arguments drawn from Quebec history.

If this historical judgment is correct, then Bills 101 and 178 are a form of redress resembling other laws of affirmative action that seek to correct age-old structures of discrimination against women or blacks, for example. These regulations may inflict a certain injustice on individuals. The debates about affirmative action in Canada and the United States have made us aware that even justified and well intended rules for hiring staff or accepting members diminish the personal rights of some individuals, as do all quota systems. For the sake of overcoming massive historical injustice society is willing to impose certain minor injustices upon a limited number of people.

Redress of historical wrongs always inflicts some suffering on the innocent. The political and cultural shift produced by the overcoming of colonial conditions always causes some damage to ordinary people, workers and farmers, who through their ethnic or linguistic heritage were associated with the once-powerful elite.

There is another, quite different, interpretation of French-English relations in Canada. I call this the federalist argument. In this case it is claimed that the effects of the British conquest and the subjugation of French Canadians have been overcome through the social contract of the 1867 Confederation. Canada, the argument proceeds, has become a dominion of equals. Quebecers are seen as a free people because the British North America Act provided adequate protection for their language and culture. From this point of view, it no longer makes sense to speak of redress or righting previous wrongs.

The people espousing the federalist argument readily admit that, in Manitoba and other provinces, the French educational system has been dismantled despite the guarantees in the British North America Act. They regret that at those historic moments the population of English Canada did not protest these political decisions. Yet the wrongs of the past, proponents argue, cannot be corrected through wrongs committed in the present by the injured party. They propose, moreover, that the exclusion of the French from the economic elite in Quebec happened mostly because French Quebecers — influenced by their leaders, especially the clergy — defined their culture in spiritual, anti-modern terms. Thus the schools of Quebec offered classical education for the elite and only rudimentary instruction for all other people. Absence of worldly ambition and lack of scientific and technical training prevented French Quebecers from climbing the social ladder during the industrialization of their society. Since the modernization brought by the Quiet Revolution has overcome this educational handicap, Quebecers have become upwardly mobile and joined the economic elite.

Seen from this perspective, it appears misguided to interpret the Quiet Revolution as part of a long anticolonial struggle. It also seems unacceptable to use redress as an appropriate category to understand the present situation.

There are important elements of truth in the federalist argument. Confederation did create legal guarantees for the survival of the French-Canadian people and their culture. Despite the limited nature of these guarantees and occasional violations, French Canadians in the province of Quebec enjoyed their own political and cultural institutions. They were not a disfranchised people like the Mexican Americans, living in the territories annexed by the United States in 1848, who received no legal recognition and enjoyed no Spanish-language institutions of their own. It is also quite true that the Catholic church defined the collective identity of French Canadians in opposition to the Protestant and secular culture of North America and hence promoted spiritual ideals and cultural institutions that would prevent assimilation.

Still in my opinion the federalist argument does not stand up. It seems to me impossible to render an account of the patterns of exclusion imposed on French Canadians without recognizing the structures of colonization operative in their society.[6]

Anglophone malaise

Redress of colonial subjugation is ethical, even if it causes some suffering to innocent people. People of modest means who are ethnically or linguistically associated with the colonial elite often suffer, though personally innocent, because they lose their sense of being at home where they live. They feel that the formerly colonized community, now liberated, accuses them of identification with the oppressor. They sometimes feel ill at ease.

I will describe the malaise felt by certain groups of anglophones and "allophones" in Quebec. The Anglo elite which exercised great power in Quebec was greatly puzzled by the Quiet Revolution. The families which set the tone in the past were pained by the new development challenging their hegemony. Yet it would be wrong harshly to judge the distinguished Westmount clique. These persons were heirs of a division of power in Quebec which they took for granted and did not question. The interrelation between unjust structures and personal responsibility is a complex ethical issue. Because the dominant culture tends to make the structures of domination invisible, it is very difficult to blame individuals who have inherited their elevated status.

Quite different is the situation of ordinary anglophone Quebecers, often working people, people without power, whose families had lived there for generations. They had felt part of Quebec society. Even though they lived at a great distance from the powerful elite and often suffered economic exploitation, the Quiet Revolution made them feel as never before that they were outsiders. They did not feel the excitement of the cultural, intellectual and artistic explosion in Quebec. The ordinary English Quebecers were often displeased by the new situation.

The shock made some English-speaking people self-critical. This happened in a variety of social contexts. Remarkable is the Black Rock Manifesto,[7] issued by a group of radical workers, which acknowledges that they had occupied the more important positions in the work force because they were English-speaking. They had been the foremen, got the office jobs, stuck together and refused to extend their solidarity to French-Canadian workers. In resounding prose the Manifesto analyses the previously unacknowledged complicity of the anglophone working class. At the same time the Manifesto also protests that now, after the Quiet Revolution, the class-conscious, francophone workers, organized in powerful unions, remain indifferent to the English-speaking members of their own class.

A scientific analysis of the Quebec labour force verifies the description presented in the Manifesto. Statistically anglophone workers and employees had held the better jobs in the province of Quebec. Again, it would be quite unjust to accuse these workers of personal wrong doing. It is only at special historical moments when people are able to see through the system where they belong and recognize the structures of subordination from which they derive some benefits.

Irish Catholics were deeply hurt by the Quebec social system. As Catholics they had belonged at the margin of English Quebec and as anglophones they were treated as marginal in the Quebec Catholic church. Often they experienced the transformation of Quebec society as an added injustice. Because of this hurt, they tended to remain outside of the extraordinary spiritual excitement experienced by the Quebec church in the sixties and seventies.

The Jewish community felt threatened by the Quiet Revolution. The European nationalist movements against the domination of the Austro-Hungarian and the Tsarist Empires had always generated anti-semitism and feelings against outsiders. In Germany the liberation struggle against the conquest of Napoleon had produced a nationalist tradition, accompanied by anti-semitism, that would eventually come to flower under German imperialism. In Quebec itself certain priests had introduced anti-semitic motifs to strengthen the people's will to survive as a distinct cultural society. This is why the Jewish community, traditionally anglophone, felt uncomfortable with French-Canadian nationalism. By contrast the 20,000 French-speaking Jews who have arrived from France and North Africa since the Quiet Revolution have felt more at home in a Quebec committed to becoming a French-speaking society.

Immigrant families from Italy, Greece, Portugal, Poland and many other countries often felt frustrated. They were led to believe that Canada was basically an English-speaking country and that French was spoken only by a minority. This was the image at one time created at the overseas consulates. These men and women who had learned one language were now expected to learn another.

A variety of groups, a variety of malaise. What is the appropriate response to these disappointments? A period of mourning over the loss of one's cultural world seems quite acceptable, maybe even necessary. Yet if the ethical reasoning presented here is correct, it seems unacceptable to resent in principle the Quiet Revolution and the self-affirmation of the French-Canadian majority. If there is room for anger, it must be directed not at French Canadians, but at the colonizing structures that humiliated them in the past and in which ordinary

anglophone Quebecers were unknowingly and innocently caught.

Many English-speaking Quebecers have got used to
the new sitution. They feel at home in Quebec, they
speak French, and they develop their English-speaking
identity in their own cultural institutions.

Asymmetrical Canada

Quite apart from the answer to the question
whether Quebecers were an oppressed people, there
is no doubt whatsoever that the relation between
French and English-speaking Canadians (whether of
British or other ethnic origin) is not a symmetrical
one. French is threatened in North America and
English is not. It is as simple as that. North America
has defined itself as an English-speaking continent.
This self-definition has produced a cultural and political trend that is still operative today. In the United
States there is new "English only" legislation directed
against Mexican Americans and other Hispanics.
Quite apart from this, since the second world war
English has become recognized as the world medium
of communication. This is partly because of the
enormous impact of American technological culture
on all continents. That Asia recognizes English as
the *lingua franca* is a heritage of the British empire.
English has become the world language of science,
technology, production and commerce. This is true
to an increasing degree even in Europe. For the first
time in world history a single language has acquired
an almost universal status.

For this and other reasons, Canada is an asym-
metrical political union. Thus the situation of the English-speaking minority in Quebec is quite different from
the francophone minorities in other provinces. In Quebec, Anglo-Canadians were a thriving, wealthy community (although there was also a disadvantaged

working class). The Anglo community built its own institutions, schools, universities, hospitals, social agencies, theatres, museums and publishing houses. A full cultural life was lived and is still being lived in English. Even the ardent nationalists of the Parti Québécois have always recognized the historical rights of the English-speaking community to its own institutions. Even as French became the language of work and of public signs, a full cultural life in English is a continuing reality in Montreal.

By contrast, the francophone minorities in the other provinces belonged to the more modest sectors of society. They could not build their own social and cultural institutions. For their survival they largely depended on the provincial goverments. French Canadians were lucky if they got their own schools. But they lacked the set of institutions required for the expression of a full cultural life. If they became lawyers, doctors, scientists, engineers or successful business people in their own province, they did this by and large not in their own language, but in English.

This lack of symmetry is etched deeply into Canadian history. Ethical reflection on the language debate must take this into account. I will mention another example of this lack of symmetry. The immigrants who arrived and still arrive in this country tend to integrate with English-speaking Canada. This is a rational thing to do on this North American continent. In the past the newcomers who arrived in Quebec sent their children to the anglophone schools. In fact if the children were not Catholic, they were obliged to go to anglophone schools. When over the last two decades Quebecers realized that the influx of immigrants was starting to reduce their majority status in the province, they introduced legislation that all newcomers to Quebec must send their children to francophone schools. Since learning the dominant North American language gives the newcomers greater economic mobility and since they sometimes have relatives in other North American cities, they would often prefer to integrate with anglophone Canadian society. It is especially hard for them if they arrive from former British colonies and hence speak English fluently. There is the possibility of mutual resentment, the newcomers against those who force their children to learn French, and Quebecers against those who — quite innocently — become Lord Durham's agents of assimilation into English-speaking Canada.

The asymmetry of Canada is such that immigrants present no threat whatever to the English language, while they do offer a challenge to French Quebecers. Of course, French Quebec has its own lively multiculturalism among the communities that come from French-speaking countries or former French colonies and mandates, such as Haitians, Lebanese, North Africans, Syrians and Vietnamese. Moreover, an ever-growing number of immigrants belonging to other ethnic communities have come to identify themselves with French Quebec. Still, the lack of symmetry that is my subject creates a special challenge for Quebec society.

Competing claims

I now return to the competing claims of collective and the personal rights. Quebecers regarded their collective right of cultural self-determination as the ethical foundation for their language charter, Bill 101. Many English-speaking Quebecers, supported by the Supreme Court of Canada, judged Bill 101 to be injurious to their personal rights, in particular to their freedom of expression. In this chapter I am examining the conflict from an ethical, not a legal point of view. Since Quebecers are a people they are indeed ethically entitled to collective self-determination. What conditions make regulations protecting collective rights at the expense of personal liberties ethically acceptable? I will argue that such regulations are ethically justified 1) if there are good and urgent reasons for them and 2) when the imposed limitations are minimal, causing only inconveniences, or when they place more considerable burdens on a very limited number of people.

For instance, the War Measures Act made the government's action during the second world war to intern and dispossess Japanese Canadians legal, but the action was unethical. Why? It was unethical because no good and urgent reason was convincingly presented and because the burden inflicted on these Canadian citizens was massive. On the other hand, I regard as ethical the decision of the Supreme Court in 1990 to defend the rule demanding forced retirement at the age of sixty-five, even though this violates personal rights protected by the Charter. According to the Supreme Court, the collective right of society to promote the public good, in this case the rejuvenation of its institutions, has here precedence over the personal rights of a limited number of people even though for some the burden may be considerable. The seat belt legislation and the RIDE program in Ontario that limit personal freedom in the name of the public good are also ethical. There are good and urgent reasons for them, and here the personal burden is minimal. I would argue the same for the legislation in English Canada that radio and television programs must have a certain percentage of Canadian content. If someone took this legislation to the Supreme Court for violating freedom of expression, the Supreme Court might possibly decide that it was unconstitutional. Still, I regard it as ethically sound because of the good and urgent reasons in its favour and because of the minimal harm done to individuals. If, on the other hand, certain parents, for religious reasons, refuse to have their children inoculated, the Supreme Court of Canada might well decide that their right of refusal is guaranteed in the Constitution. I would argue on ethical grounds, following the principles set out here, that for the sake of the public good the government should invoke the "notwithstanding clause" and override the Court's decision.

Before getting to Quebec's Bill 101, I will look at a case in another country that has a certain similarity with our situation. Newspapers have reported that the republic of Estonia in the Soviet Union has introduced strict legislation to make Estonian the language of work and public life. The law intends to protect the survival of the Estonian people. Since the Estonian republic is industrially developed, it has received an enormous influx of workers and others from other parts of the Soviet Union who speak Russian as their working language and who on the whole refuse to learn Estonian. It would appear that today only sixty percent of the population is still Estonian-speaking. In this situation the Estonian government has decided — against the wishes of the government in Moscow — to introduce a strict legislation that makes Estonian the public language and demands that it be learned by all people working in factories and offices. According to the newspaper account, people are given four years to learn Estonian. The new law is experienced as a great burden by many people, especially by the Russians whose families have lived in Estonia for centuries.

I know too little about the historical situation to ask serious ethical questions. Since the Soviet government is authoritarian and russification has been promoted all over the Soviet Union, the western reader tends to have sympathy with the Estonians. But since they have been reduced to only sixty percent of the population — Quebec is over eighty percent francophone — the question is whether such a law can be enforced. Can any legislation reverse such a massive trend?

Bill 101

What about the ethical foundation of Bill 101? In a McGill University publication, *The Reporter*,[8] I have defended the position that the bill is ethically acceptable because the two conditions are fulfilled: good and urgent reasons, and minimal personal limitation.

That there are good and urgent reasons for legal measures to protect French language and culture cannot be in doubt. Anglo-American technological culture is an omnipresent challenge. But what about public signs in French only? French Quebecers argue that unless the province's public face, especially in Montreal, is visibly and unmistakably French, the English-speaking communities and recent arrivals will think of Quebec as a bilingual society. It is true that many anglophones, especially the supporters of the Equality Party, oppose the idea of a French-speaking Quebec, even though the historic rights of their own institutions are recognized and protected. What these citizens want is a bilingual Quebec. In my own judgment, the above-mentioned asymmetry in Canadian society is such that bilingualism in Quebec would encourage immigrants to seek integration with the anglophone community and thus weaken the francophone majority: bilingualism in Quebec would open the door in other ways to the gradual take-over by the powerful, culturally dominant, omnipresent North American language.

More difficult from an ethical point of view is the second question whether the limitations imposed by Bill 101 on anglophones and "allophones" are minimal. Do public signs in French cause only certain inconveniences? Or is the sign legislation insulting?

The Supreme Court looked upon the question simply from the legal point of view. Freedom of expression, a fundamental human right, is here understood as extending to commercial signs. The first purpose of freedom of expression was of course to make democracy possible, that is to allow public disagreement in the sphere of religion, ethics and politics. The extension of this freedom to commercial signs is recent. Thus a Canadian Court rejected the plea that advertising directed at children under thirteen be prohibited. I regretted this decision even though it was made in the name of freedom of expression. How will the courts rule when the producers of spirituous liquors plead before them that the law forbidding them to advertise is unconstitutional? Whatever the courts decide, it would seem, from an ethical point of view, that the freedom to communicate on commercial signs is not an essential part of the freedom of expression.

More serious is the argument given by some English-speaking Quebecers that the sign legislation of Bill 101 and the present Bill 178 is insulting. This is an ethical argument. People have the right to be respected. Their human dignity demands recognition. Why do many anglophones regard the sign legislation as insulting? I do not suggest that the reason is a resentment-laden oversensitivity caused by the loss of their position of privilege. In this chapter, I presume good faith on all sides of the argument.

Professor William Tetley of the McGill Law Faculty has proposed the idea that anglophone and francophone Canadians have slightly different moral sensitivities.[9] The British tradition and Anglo North American practice have always emphasized personal human rights while the continental European traditions and French Canadians had a much stronger sense of people's collective rights. Behind these traditions are different perceptions of the state, on the one hand the liberal view that the role of the state is confined to protecting the rights of property and civil liberties, and on the other the more traditional view that the role of the state includes the promotion of culture and the common good. These different political philosophies have been generated by different historical experiences. It is perhaps the keen sense of civil liberties mediated by the British-North American tradition that makes some Anglo Quebecers feel that the present sign legislation is offensive.

At the same time, the preoccupation with personal rights can become obsessive. Some North Americans actually believe that medicare and interventionist economic policies violate the freedom of individuals. Occasionally angry citizens even argue that the seat belt legislation is fascist, at odds with the democratic freedoms.

There may be another reason why some English-speaking Quebecers find the language legislation insulting. An inconvenience is offensive when we detect behind it a lack of respect. When we line up at the airport waiting to be searched electronically, the inconvenience does not insult us. We recognize that this measure protects us. When we have to wait endlessly at the bank, we sometimes get angry because we believe, rightly or wrongly, that the bank does not respect its customers and, despite its high profits, refuses to hire enough personnel. We find a gesture insulting when we interpret it as part of an effort to diminish us. Some English-speaking Quebecers find the sign legislation insulting because they see it as an attempt by French Quebecers to teach them a lesson and to get even with them, innocent though they be, for humiliations inflicted in the past.

Anglophone Quebecers who admire the Quiet Revolution and sympathize with Quebec's historical project do not find the sign legislation insulting, even when it is occasionally inconvenient. These anglophones are confident that if they speak French and recognize French as the public language, they can live a creative cultural life in English in their own community with its great institutions, including universities and theatres.

What about the solidarity rights?

The more serious issue that worries many progressive Quebecers, francophone and anglophone, is the growing indifference of society to the so-called solidarity rights: the rights of workers and the powerless to organize and demand that their just claims be recognized by the powerful. The debate about the conflict between personal and collective rights remains defective if it does not include concern for economic justice.

What has happened in Quebec during the last ten years is the arrival of the world-wide phenomenon, the new, monetarist orientation of capitalism, characterized by the widening gap between rich and poor, the increase of unemployment and job insecurity, the decline of industrial employment, the shift to low-paying, low-skill jobs in the service sector, the feminization of poverty, the housing shortage, the roaming of the destitute in the streets and the hopelessness of ever-growing crowds of young people.

In Quebec as in other parts of the world, the left — the traditional defender of solidarity rights — has been decimated. The Parti Québécois has dropped its social democratic agenda. The Quebec N.D.P is very small; it is still trying to adjust to the new situation. The radical parties and movements of the past have all disappeared. Many of the formerly left-wing intellectuals at the universities have turned to a post-modern interpretation of society, which looks upon social movements for structural change as useless and illusory. The Quebec newspapers have largely abandoned their role as social critics which they played so well in the past.

The surviving left in Quebec, though nationalist, is increasingly suspicious of the nationalism advocated by the two leading political parties and prominent members of the business community. What will happen to the workers, the unemployed and people on welfare in the new Quebec? The reason why the left always stood up for Quebec's language and culture was to defend the collectivist values and the spirit of solidarity characteristic of the old Catholic Quebec, attitudes that might now, in secular form, become a bulwark against the individualism and competitive spirit of capitalist North America. The left is worried whenever nationalist goals are not joined to the socialist aim of economic justice.

Chapter Seven

The Bishops
and
Quebec Nationalism

The massive secularization produced by the Quiet Revolution made practising Catholics into a minority in Quebec.[1] The Catholic bishops decided not to react to this situation with resentment. To find new ways of serving the Catholic community, they created the Dumont Commission whose task it was to report on the new religious situation and make recommendations for innovative pastoral approaches.[2] Since the church had been identified with *le peuple canadien* from the beginning, the bishops promised they would continue to walk with this people, share its concerns and respond from a Catholic perspective to the problems that emerged in its history. The bishops came to respect the pluralistic character of Quebec society and recognized that they represented a minority. Still, they would make their contributions to the public debate from a Catholic point of view.

Over the years the bishops have followed this policy. For decades their pastoral letters have dealt with the important public issues discussed in Quebec society. Their perspective on these issues was defined by their solidarity with the groups that bore the heaviest burdens in society: the workers, the unemployed, welfare recipients, and especially women, poor immigrants and refugees. In the language of political science, the bishops' perspective was that of the democratic left.

This shift to the left corresponds to the evolution of Catholic social teaching during the sixties and seventies. The ethical commitment to look upon society from the perspective of its weakest members, the so-called "option for the poor," was first endorsed by the Latin American church. It was later supported in papal teaching, especially John Paul II's *Laborem exercens* and it became particularly fruitful in the social teaching of the Canadian bishops. Best known among many pastoral letters on social justice is the bishops' 1983 statement, "Ethical Reflections on the Economic Crisis," which offered an extended ethical critique of contemporary capitalism.[3] The Quebec bishops, active in the caucus of the Canadian bishops, worked among themselves and produced their own pastorals addressed to Quebec Catholics.

How did the Quebec bishops respond to the new nationalism generated by the Quiet Revolution? This is my topic in this chapter. I will not deal with the church's relation to the conservative, anti-modern, xenophobic nationalism supported by prominent clergymen in Quebec prior to the second world war.[4] Nor will I discuss the response of the bishops to the recent national self-affirmation of Native peoples. To assess the bishops' reaction to contemporary Quebec nationalism I will examine the pastoral letters during the last two decades, especially the two most pertinent, "The Charter of the French Language," a 1977 response to the White Paper published by the Parti Québécois government introducing Bill 101, and "The people of Quebec and its political future," issued in 1979 before the referendum.

The people of Quebec

The bishops strongly defend the position that Quebecers constitute a people and that as such they have the right to self-determination. Already in 1967, the pastoral statement produced by the Canadian bishops, anglophone and francophone, on the occasion of Canada's hundredth anniversary,[5] clearly acknowledged the peoplehood of French Canadians. At this time the other Christian Churches made public statements thanking God for the first century of Confederation and asking for God's blessing on the next century. By contrast the Catholic bishops could not get away with a short statement. They found themselves obliged to produce a long and partly critical letter analysing both the strengths and weaknesses of the Canadian Confederation.

According to this 1967 document, "the chief malady of Canadian society" was the growing discontent felt by French Canadians over the many obstacles that hinder them from affirming their identity and developing their culture. To help Canadians understand this situation, the document explained that "the French-Canadian community is a linguistic and cultural group with roots three centuries old in the soil of Canada, the soil which has served as the 'cradle of their life, labour, sorrow and dreams.' Here is a people . . . vividly aware that they make up a community enjoying a unity, individuality and spirit of their own, all of which yield them an unshakable right to their own existence and development."[6] The document said that this is why French Quebecers keep referring to themselves as "a nation," even though this vocabulary leads to serious misunderstandings with English-speaking Canadians.

In the pastoral letter "The people of Quebec and its political future,"[7] written before the referendum, the Quebec bishops strongly defended the right of Quebecers to cultural and political self-determination, giving a highly nuanced definition of peoplehood. The bishops argued that the evolving moral sense of the world community, especially as expressed at the United Nations, has come to recognize the right of peoples to define their own future in cultural, economic and political terms. The bishops argued that the Christian churches have endorsed this developing moral sense. This collective right, they noted, is not a legal assurance laid down in a book of law: it is rather an ethical right that entitles a people to act collectively on behalf of its own future.

At the same time the bishops insisted that it was not their task to tell Quebecers how to shape their political future whether within or without the federal system. It is the people who must choose. The church has no mandate to influence a political decision of this kind. The church's task, as the bishops see it, is to defend Quebec's right to self-determination and to offer ethical principles that should guide such a political venture. While the bishops never mentioned the word "nationalism," their pastoral statements provided a set of norms to help Catholics discern what kind of nationalism is ethically acceptable.

The first question to be answered is who belongs to the Quebec people? Only French Quebecers? Already in their 1977 pastoral, "The Charter of the French Language," the bishops answered this question in a manner that discouraged ethnic nationalism.[8] Quebecers, they argue, are the people who live in Quebec: the French majority, of course, but also the Native peoples with roots in the distant past, the English-speaking community long established in Quebec and the ethno-cultural communities who have arrived more recently. It is together with these groups that the ethnically-French majority constitutes the Quebec people.

The point is made again in the 1979 pastoral, "The people of Quebec and its future": "It is together with these groups that the francophone people of Quebec today ponder their future and search for an answer."[9] Ethically acceptable nationalism, according to the bishops, is defined in territorial, not in ethnic terms. "The future of Quebec shall not be decided by the francophone majority alone, but by all its citizens, that is by all who live within its boundaries, develop its economy, form a significant community, enrich its common culture, share the same legal and political institutions inherited from a common history. It is in this sense then, providing for all the necessary nuances, that one may refer to 'the people of Quebec.'"[10]

This was a significant development. In their 1967 statement, the Canadian bishops still proposed an idea of peoplehood defined in ethnic terms. Quebecers were descendants and heirs of the French-Canadian community founded over three centuries earlier. In 1979, over ten years later, the Quebec bishops recognized that this definition was no longer adequate. They resisted the idea of an ethnic nationalism. According to them, history has taught the founding community of French origin to interact with Native peoples and groups of other ethnic origins and to construct with them — not always without injustice and conflict — a modern society, which is the Quebec of today. Today the nationhood of Quebec, the distinct society, must be defined in territorial terms.

In the same pastoral, the bishops offered further reflections on the conditions which make nationalism ethically acceptable. A nationalist movement for political self-determination is ethical only if it recognizes the interdependence of all nations and envisages a political future of trust and co-operation with them. Excluded is an isolationist political imagination. Secondly, a nationalist movement is ethically acceptable only if it respects minority communities and guarantees their human rights.

In this context as in several others, the bishops lamented the presence of prejudice and discriminatory practices in their society. The churchmen recognized that the passion engendered by the struggle for collective self-determination easily leads to conflicts with those who are seen as obstacles and often encourages insulting discourse, ethnically-based prejudice, and discriminatory practices. Social ethics and elementary Christian teaching, the bishops argued, demand that this trend be vehemently resisted.

To calm the rhetoric used in the debate prior to the referendum, the bishops told the Catholic community that in the debate over federalism or independence no one may invoke the Gospel to defend his or her point of view. It would be wrong to say that Confederation is a holy covenant and that to disrupt it would be a grave sin. It would be equally wrong to say that the subjugation of Quebec is so massive that to oppose its independence would be sinful. The crucial ethical issue, according to the bishops, is not whether Quebec chooses one political option or the other, but rather whether the political project chosen will conform to the norms of social and economic justice.

The language legislation

How have the bishops of Quebec reacted to Bill 101, the charter of the French Language, which the Parti Québécois introduced in 1977? The bishops regarded this historical event as so important that they decided to comment on it in a pastoral letter. They examined the ethical questions raised by the new legislation.

Relying on the White Paper produced by the government to announce the new bill, the bishops spelled out the intentions of the new law and in general approved of the values that the law wanted to promote. The bishops agreed that the French language needed protection. "To achieve this, the bill intends to redress the equilibrium between the majority and the minority and make Quebec a basically French-speaking society.

Among the measures taken to assure this will be principally the proclamation of French as the official language of Quebec, the common language of our joint social project, including the means to assure its implementation: in the life of society, in teaching, communications, the work place, administration, the face of Quebec, etc."[11]

Is this just? The new bill would limit certain acquired rights of the English-speaking minority and affect the immigration of other ethno-cultural communities. The moral justification for restricting these rights, the bishops argued, is redress of a previous unbalance, the correction of an unjust situation. "It has become increasingly evident that justice should be established in favour of the francophone majority which, because of certain historical circumstances, did not receive what was rightly due to them, for instance protection, security, economic participation corresponding to their number, recognition and promotion of the cultural values of their language."[12]

At the same time redress demanded by justice has ethical limits. What is required is the discovery of the right proportion between the rights of the majority and those of the minorities. "The concern of the francophone community to see the priority of French respected must not prompt it to limit excessively the use of English."[13] The bishops were pleased that the White Paper contained declarations such as these: "English will always have an important place in Quebec. . . . English belongs to the cultural heritage of Quebecers. . . . That English-speaking Quebecers keep their language, their ways of life and their culture is held by the government as a given of our common history."[14] It is true that none of the nationalist politicians in the Parti Québécois have ever questioned the historic rights of the English-speaking community to its educational, social and cultural institutions such as schools, universities, hospitals and welfare agencies.

While the bishops approved of Bill 101 in principle, they worried that its application might manifest lack of respect for minorities. The bishops defined Quebec as a multi-ethnic society. They demanded that the francophone majority never forget that anglophones and "allophones" are Quebecers, members of the same political community, citizens enjoying the same rights, with whom the majority participate in the building of society.

The ruling of the Supreme Court of Canada in December 1988 that certain articles of Bill 101 — especially the one demanding commercial signs in French only — were not in comformity with the Quebec Charter of Rights produced a heated debate in Quebec. For French Quebecers Bill 101 was a charter as much as the Charter of Rights. English-speaking Quebecers did not agree. Eventually the Liberal government decided to find a compromise solution. Invoking the "notwithstanding clause" of the Canadian Constitution to limit the application of the Supreme Court decision, Premier Robert Bourassa introduced Bill 178, which allowed bilingual commercial signs inside the stores but ruled that commercial signs facing the street had to be in French only. Because Mr. Bourassa had promised to permit bilingual signs before his election, the anglophone community felt betrayed by the government's decision. Many anglophones did not fully appreciate his dilemma. If he had scaled down the protection of Montreal's French public face, great numbers of Quebecers would have turned to the separatist Parti Québécois.

A group of English-speaking Catholics, unhappy with the government's action, addressed a formal request to the Quebec bishops, asking them to offer an ethical evaluation of the Bill 178 and the use of the "notwithstanding clause." The bishops replied to this request in a public declaration on the need for civic friendship.[15] They argued that a court decision based on an interpretation of existing laws is not necessarily decisive for an ethical evaluation. Ethical reflection on Bill 178 and even on Bill 101 must take into account the concern of the two linguistic communities, both of which are minorities in different ways and both of which are or feel threatened in different degrees. In the earlier 1977 pastoral letter, the bishops already acknowledged that the redress of a previous imbalance in favour of the francophone majority places certain restrictions on the anglophone community. This, alas, is the logic of redress. In their declaration twelve years later, the bishops still thought that in Quebec French remains threatened by the powerful language of the North American continent. French still needs supplementary protection.

The Supreme Court understood the situation as a conflict between the collective right of Quebec to promote the French language and the civil liberties of English-speaking Quebecers, particularly their freedom of expression on commercial signs. The bishops saw this dilemma rather differently as a conflict between two collective rights, the group rights of francophones versus the group rights of anglophones. The question the bishops asked, therefore, is whether Bills 101 and 178 threatened the well-being of the language and the cultural life enjoyed by the anglophone community. Because they answer this question in the negative, they defend the ethical character of the French language charter.

Social and economic justice

Much more important than the language question is the issue of social and economic justice. I mentioned above the turn to the left taken by the bishops of Quebec and Canada in the seventies. Over the years, the bishops have become constant critics of the governments at Ottawa and at Quebec for their growing indifference to the well-being of working people and the fate of men and women whose lives are damaged by the never-ending economic crisis. While the church in the past repeatedly repudiated socialism, in the seventies the Canadian bishops acknowledged socialism as a valid option for Catholics if they tried to promote the ethics of Jesus within the socialist movement.[16] A reading of the book, *La justice sociale comme bonne nouvelle*, the collection of the Quebec bishops' pastoral statements over a decade, reveals the extent of their social solidarity. These pastoral letters deal with specific labour struggles, the unemployed, health at the work place, the co-operative movement, unemployed youth, people on welfare, the closing of factories, immigrant workers, the threat to the environment, the problems of farmers and the decline of the regions.

The bishops not only blame the government and its political philosophy, they also denounce the injustices committed by other Quebec agencies, particularly the discrimination inflicted on immigrants and their families. Because the bishops envisage Quebec as a pluri-ethnic society, they are disturbed by the existence of widespread prejudice and particularly by the economic exploitation connected with it.

In one pastoral letter,[17] the bishops expressed a particular concern for the exploitation of immigrant women, especially in the clothing industry, in hotels and restaurants and in domestic work and other family services. The bishops asked Quebecers to reflect on the situation of these immigrant women, some of whom find themselves in the labour market for the first time. They have problems with personal adaptation; they find it difficult to re-organize their family lives and develop a new type of relationship with their husbands; they lack access to day care services. In addition to these serious problems, the bishops continued, we inflict upon them our mistrust, our hesitation and our prejudices. In this context as in many others the bishops insisted that "the society we are about to build, whatever the political form we give to it, must be open, welcoming and solidary."[18]

The bishops never use the word "nationalism." Instead, they speak of Quebec's quest for political self-determination. Their message is here quite clear. A nationalist movement is ethically acceptable only if it is guided by a vision of a just society. And what is a just society? In a second pastoral letter prior to the referendum, called "Building Together a Better Society,"[19] the bishops spelled out their vision of the just society under several categories: a society of participation, a society based on respect for human rights and acknowledgment of civil duties, a society based on a just distribution of goods and responsibilities, a society attentive to cultural and spiritual values and finally a society that is open and solidary.

The bishops made the same point in their brief submitted to the Bélanger-Campeau Commission on the political and constitutional future of Quebec. They were disturbed that "the national question" has been increasingly separated from "the social question," the question of social and economic justice. If justice to workers, the unemployed and the poor becomes a secondary issue on Quebec's political agenda, society will drift further in an ethically reprehensible direction.

The teaching of the Quebec bishops on the nationalist movement recalls the theory relating ethics and nationalism presented over half a century ago by the German Protestant theologian Paul Tillich. In his 1932 book, *The Socialist Decision*,[20] Tillich argued against liberal and socialist thinkers who in the name of universal values rejected nationalism in any of its forms. Because of their exclusive reliance on reason, he believed, liberals and socialists underestimated the important role played by particular national traditions in the building of a just and co-operative society. Tillich admitted, of course, that the unguarded surrender to a particular national tradition, whether defined in religious, cultural or ethnic terms, represented a dangerous political orientation because its values, however precious, can quickly become principles of discrimination, exclusion and subjugation. This danger is the element of truth in liberal and socialist theory. Still, the values mediated through family, tribe, community, church or nation are so deeply woven into people's personal and communal lives that it would be foolish to adopt a social philosophy that disregards the national heritage altogether. Tillich criticized the "economism" of liberal and socialist thinkers, i.e. their tendency to analyse society in purely economic terms, either — for liberals — as a product created by the logic of the market or — for socialists — as a reflection of economically defined class conflict. Sound socialist policy, Tillich argued in this book, would be to appreciate particular cultural, ethnic and religious values, including nationalist sentiment, which are capable of creating solidarity and social cohesion, provided that their particularism was subject to the universal principles of justice. Tillich's theory resembles the Quebec bishops' positions during the past two decades. A nationalist movement, or national self-affirmation, is considered an ethical undertaking if it is directed by a vision of society defined in terms of justice, equality, respect and participation.

Notes

Chapter One
Catholicism and Secularization in Quebec

[1] Canadian Catholic Conference, "On the Occasion of the Hundredth Year of Confederation," in *Do Justice! The Social Teaching of the Canadian Catholic Bishops*, ed. E.F. Sheridan (Toronto: The Jesuit Centre for Social Faith and Justice, and Sherbrooke: Éditions Paulines, 1987), p. 126.

[2] Cf. William Ryan, *The Clergy and the Economic Growth of Quebec* (Quebec: Presses de l'Université Laval, 1966).

[3] Philippe Garigue, "French Canadian Kinship and Urban Life," in *French Canadian Society*, ed. M. Rioux and Y. Martin (Toronto: McClelland & Stewart, 1964), pp. 358-372.

[4] I have followed the distinction between industrial and political modernization, defined and applied in D. Posgate and K. McRoberts, *Quebec: Social Change and Political Crisis* (Toronto: McClelland & Stewart, 1976). This excellent book has been my guide in analysing the evolution of Quebec society.

[5] J.C. Falardeau, "The Role and Importance of the Church in French Canada," in M. Rioux and Y. Martin, *op. cit.*, pp. 342-357.

[6] Cf. Léon Dion, *Le Bill 60 et la société québécoise* (Montreal: H.M.H., 1967).

[7] Everett Hughes, *French Canada in Transition* (Chicago: University of Chicago Press, 1943).

[8] John Porter, *The Vertical Mosaic* (Toronto: University of Toronto Press, 1965), pp. 91-98.

[9] *Report of the Royal Commission on Bilingualism and Biculturalism*, vol. iii, pp. 447-469.

[10] Cf. D. Posgate and K. McRoberts, *op. cit.*, pp. 102-109.

[11] Cf. Gérard Dion and Louis O'Neil, *Le chrétien et les élections* (Montreal: Éditions de l'Homme, 1960).

[12] *Les insolences du Frère Untel* (Montreal: Éditions de l'Homme, 1960).

[13] Raymond Lemieux, "Les catholiques," *Le Devoir*, April 8, 1982, p. 22. The article is part of a special section dealing with the church in Quebec.

[14] The Dumont Commission published several volumes in 1971. The last volumes came out in 1972. See footnotes 9, 10 and 11 of Chapter Two.

[15] David Martin, *A General Theory of Secularization* (Oxford: Blackwell, 1978).

[16] *Ibid.*, pp. 28-29.

[17] Ibid., pp. 42-43. Also consult Martin's index on Ireland, Poland and Belgium.

[18] Cf. J.C. Falardeau, *op. cit.*

[19] For a useful analysis of culture and religion in the context of the Quebec labour movement, see P.E. Trudeau, "The Province of Quebec at the Time of the Asbestos Strike," in *The Asbestos Strike*, ed. P.E. Trudeau (Toronto: James, Lewis & Samuel, 1974), pp. 1-84.

[20] *L'Église et le mouvement ouvrier au Québec* (Montreal: Centre de pastorale en milieu ouvrier, no date).

[21] Gérard Dion, "The Church and the Conflict in the Asbestos Industry," in P.E. Trudeau, *op. cit.*, pp. 205-225.

[22] A.J. Bélanger, *L'apoliticisme des idéologies québécoises: 1934-1936* (Quebec: Presses de l'Université Laval, 1974); D. Monière, *Le développement des idéologies au Québec: 1827-1959* (Montreal: Parti-Pris, 1977).

[23] For the role and importance of corporatism in Quebec, see A.J. Bélanger, *op. cit.*, pp. 307-327.

[24] P.E. Trudeau, *op. cit.*, pp. 9-13.

[25] G. Baum, *Catholics and Canadian Socialism* (Toronto: Lorimer, 1980 and New York: Paulist Press, 1981), pp. 175-188.

[26] A.J. Bélanger, *Ruptures et constantes: Les idéologies du Québec en éclatement* (Montreal: H.M.H., 1977), pp. 65-135.

[27] Paul Longpré, "L'Église dépouillée de ses pouvoirs," in *Une certaine révolution tranquille* (Montreal: La Presse, 1975). For a study of the secularization of a single parish see C. Moreux, *Fin d'une religion?* (Montreal: Presses de l'Université de Montréal, 1969).

[28] See note 12 above.

[29] See note 6 above.

[30] Cf. Lise D'Ambroise, "Confessionalité scolaire: Vingt ans de débats politiques," *Relations* (May 1981): 145-158.

[31] *L'Université dit non aux Jésuites* (Montreal: Éditions de l'Homme, 1961).

[32] "Des chrétiens parlent du Front Commun," *Vie ouvrière*, 105 (May 1976).

[33] See *Relations*, January 1979, pp. 3-5.

Chapter Two
The Dumont Report:
Democratizing the Catholic Church

[1] *Lumen Gentium*, nn. 12, 37, *The Documents of Vatican II*, ed. W. Abbott (New York: Herder and Herder, 1966), pp. 26-30, 64-65.

[2] *Ibid.*, nn. 22, 23, *The Documents of Vatican II*, pp. 43-45.

[3] See, for instance, *Sollicitudo rei socialis* (1987), n. 15. One paragraph reads: "It must be again restated that no special group, for example a political party, has the right to usurp the role of sole leader, since this brings about the destruction of the true subjectivity of society and of the individual citizens, as happens in every form of totalitarianism. In this situation the individual and the people become 'objects, in spite of all the declarations to the contrary.'" *The Logic of Solidarity*, ed. G. Baum and R. Ellesberg (Maryknoll, N.Y.: Orbis Books, 1989), p. 14.

[4] Cf. World Synod of Bishops, "Justicia in mundo" (1971), nn. 39-48 in *The Gospel of Peace and Justice*, ed. J. Gremillion (Maryknoll, N.Y.: Orbis Books, 1976), pp. 522-523; Latin American Bishops Conference, "Final Document" (1979), nn. 659-720, in *Puebla and Beyond*, ed. J. Eagleson and P. Scharper (Maryknoll, N.Y.: Orbis Books, 1979), pp. 215-222; Bishops of the United States, "Economic Justice for All" (1986), n. 358, in *Origins* 16 (November 27, 1986): 447.

[5] Cf. Thomas Bruneau, *The Church in Brazil: The Politics of Religion* (Austin: University of Texas Press, 1982); Scott Mainwaring, *The Catholic Church and Politics in Brazil: 1916-1985* (Stanford: Stanford University Press, 1986).

[6] For reference to the Puebla Document, see note 4 above.

[7] Francis McDonagh, "Rome and the Brazilian Church," *The Month* 22 (June 1989): 215-222.

[8] See Chapter One of this book.

[9] *L'Église du Québec: un héritage, un projet* (Montreal: Fides, 1971).

[10] Nive Voisine et al, *Histoire de l'Église catholique au Québec, 1608-1970* (Montreal: Fides, 1971); Norman Wener and Jocelyne Bernier, *Croyants du Canada français — I: recherches sur les attitudes et les modes d'appartenance* (Montreal: Fides, 1971).

[11] Gabriel Clément, *Histoire de l'Action catholique au Canada français* (Montreal: Fides, 1972); Norman Wener and Jacques Champagne, *Croyants du Canada français — II: Des opinions et des attentes* (Montreal: Fides, 1972); Yves-M. Coté, *L'Église du Québec: un héritage, un projet — Rapport synthèse: instrument de travail* (Montreal: Fides, 1972).

[12] Guy Rocher, *Entre les rêves et l'histoire* (Montreal: VLB, 1989), pp. 139-159.

[13] *L'Église du Québec, op. cit.*, pp. 43-44.

[14] *Ibid.*, pp. 52-59.

[15] *Ibid.*, p. 85.

[16] *Ibid.*, p. 103.

[17] *Ibid.*, pp. 64-68.

[18] *Ibid.*, pp. 86-90.

[19] *Ibid.*, pp. 63-75.

[20] *Ibid.*, pp. 90-92.

[21] *Ibid.*, pp. 129-137.

[22] *Ibid.*, pp. 138-150.

[23] *Ibid.*, p. 131.

[24] *Ibid.*, pp. 114-128.

[25] *Ibid.*, p. 95.

[26] *Ibid.*, p. 114.

[27] *Ibid.*, p. 115.

[28] *Ibid.*, p. 196.

[29] *Ibid.*, p. 134.

[30] *Ibid.*, p. 135.

[31] *Ibid.*, p. 112.

[32] *Ibid.*, pp. 257-289. In an appendix (pp. 295-303) the report proposes a detailed plan for financing the recommended institutional changes.

[33] *Ibid.*, p. 259.

[34] *Ibid.,* pp. 266-267.

[35] *Ibid.,* pp. 260-264.

[36] *Ibid.,* pp. 268-273.

[37] *Ibid.,* pp. 274-280.

[38] *Ibid.,* pp. 281-289.

[39] "Le peuple québécois et son avenir politique," *La justice sociale comme bonne nouvelle: Messages sociaux, économiques et politiques des évêques du Québec, 1972-1983* (Montreal: Bellarmin, 1984), pp. 137-144.

Chapter Three
Politisés Chrétiens:
A Christian-Marxist Network in Quebec, 1974-1982

[1] This development has been analysed in G. Baum, *Theology and Society* (New York: Paulist Press, 1987), pp. 3-31.

[2] *Ibid.,* pp. 15-16.

[3] Ulrich Duchrow, *Global Economy* (Geneva: WCC Publications, 1987), pp. 70-83.

[4] E.F. Sheridan, ed., *Do Justice! The Social Teaching of the Canadian Bishops* (Toronto: Jesuit Centre for Social Faith and Justice, 1987), p. 199.

[5] Pablo Richard, "Political Organizations of Christians in Latin America: From Christian Democracy to a New Model," *The Church and Christian Democracy,* eds. G. Baum and J. Coleman, *Concilium,* vol 193 (Edinburgh: T. & T. Clark, 1987), pp. 14-26.

[6] Gabriel Clément, "La Crise de 1966," *Histoire de l'Action catholique au Canada français* (Montreal: Fides, 1972), pp. 288-306.

[7] Jean-Guy Vaillancourt, "Les groupes socio-politiques progressistes dans le catholicisme québécois contemporain," *Les mouvements religieux aujourd'hui: théories et pratiques,* ed. Jean-Paul Rouleau, *Les Cahiers du CRSR,* vol. 5 (Montreal: Bellarmin, 1984).

[8] *Relations* 30 (May 1970): 131-155.

[9] Guy Paiement, *Renouveau communautaire au Québec: Expérience nouvelle* (Montreal: Fides, 1974).

[10] *Relations* 30 (November 1970): 297.

[11] *Relations* 31 (May 1971): 139-144.

[12] *Relations* 31 (May 1971): 146; Jules Girardi, *Amour chrétien et violence révolutionnaire* (Paris: Cerf, 1970).

[13] Yves Vaillancourt, "Quelques questions à une lettre de Paul VI," *Relations* 31 (June 1971): 174-177.

[14] *Relations* 31 (July/August 1971): 207.

[15] *Relations* 31 (September 1971): 239.

[16] Cf. J. Rouillard, *Histoire de la CSN: 1927-1981* (Montreal: Boréal Express/CSN, 1981), p. 240.

[17] *Relations* 32 (January 1972).

[18] *Relations* 32 (May 1972): 141-145.

[19] Guy Bourgeault, "Un réseau qui se bâtit," *Relations* 32 (May 1972): 142.

[20] *Relations* 32 (June 1972): 176-180. For a detailed documentation of this movement, see John Eagleson, ed., *Christians and Socialism: Documentation of the Christians for Socialism Movement in Latin America* (Maryknoll, N.Y.: Orbis, 1976).

[21] *Prêtres et laïcs* 23 (November 1973): 533-553.

[22] *Relations* 34 (November 1974): 293.

[23] *Ibid.,* pp. 293-297. This November issue of *Relations* titled "Les chrétiens dans le mouvement ouvrier au Québec," the most radical issue ever published by the review, contains several documents emanating from the Réseau.

[24] *Relations* 35 (June 1975): 174-176.

[25] *Ibid.,* 32 (January 1972).

[26] "A Society to be Transformed," *Do Justice!* ed. E.F. Sheridan (Toronto: Jesuit Centre for Social Faith and Justice, 1987), p. 331, n. 15.

[27] *Ibid.,* p. 332, n. 18.

[28] See chapter 1 in this book, pp. 38-47

[29] The Report on Cap-Rouge, *Vie ouvrière* 25 (January 1975): especially 34.

[30] Editorial by Paul-Émile Charland, *Vie ouvrière* 26 (August 1976): 198-200. See the three special issues of *Vie ouvrière* 28: "Hommes de peine et femmes de ménage" (January 1978); "Les travailleurs immigrants" (February 1978); and "Les vieux nous racontent" (March, 1978).

[31] For a brief account of this development, see Monique Dumais, Louise Melançon, Marie-Andrée Roy, "Dix ans déjà," *L'autre parole* 30 (June 1986): 4-6.

[32] *Vie ouvrière* 27 (December 1977): 589-593.

[33] *Relations* 39 (September 1979): 234-237.

[34] *Ibid.*, pp. 238-242.

[35] For the famous text on "the preferential option for the poor" and the need for conversion, promulgated in 1979 by the Latin American Bishops Conference at Puebla, Mexico, see the "Final Document," nn. 1134-40, in John Eagleson & P. Sharper, eds., *Puebla and Beyond* (Maryknoll, N.Y.: Orbis, 1979), p. 264.

[36] *Vie ouvrière* 29 (March 1979): 195-196.

[37] See the reports by Raymond Levac, "La rencontre des militants du monde ouvrier du Québec," *Vie ouvrière* 29 (June/July 1979): 329-332, and "L'Église qui naît de la classe ouvrière," *Vie ouvrière* 29 (June/ July 1979): 368-373.

Chapter Four
Jacques Grand'Maison: Prophecy and Politics

[1] Jacques Grand'Maison, *La nouvelle classe et l'avenir du Québec* (Montréal: Éditions Alain Stanké, 1979).

[2] Jacques Grand'Maison, *Au seuil critique d'un nouvel âge* (Montreal: Éditions Léméac, 1979).

[3] Cf. Jacques Grand'Maison, *Nouveaux modèles sociaux et développements* (Montreal: Hurtubise, 1972), pp. 460-462.

[4] *Laborem exercens*, n. 20, in G. Baum, *The Priority of Labor* (New York: Paulist Press, 1982), pp. 134-137.

[5] "A Declaration on Social and Economic Policy Directions for Canada by Members of Popular Sector Groups," produced by the Working Committee on Social Solidarity and published by *Our Times*, Toronto, 390 Dufferin St., Toronto, Ont., 1987.

[6] Jacques Grand'Maison, *Au mitan de la vie* (Montreal: Éditions Léméac, 1976).

[7] Jacques Grand'Maison, *Crise de prophétisme* (Montreal: L'Action catholique canadienne, 1965).

[8] Jacques Grand'Maison, *Stratégies sociales et nouvelles idéologies* (Montreal: Hurtubise, 1971).

[9] Puebla: Latin American Bishops Conference, "The Final Document," par. 536, *Puebla and Beyond*, eds. J. Eagleson and P. Scharper (Maryknoll, N.Y.: Orbis Books, 1979), p. 198.

[10] *Ibid.*, pp. 199-200.

[11] *Ibid.*, p. 198.

[12] John Paul II, *Sollicitudo rei socialis*, n. 41, G. Baum and R. Ellsberg, *The Logic of Solidarity* (Maryknoll, N.Y.: Orbis Books, 1989), p. 45.

[13] *Quadragesimo anno*, par. 77, in *Seven Great Encyclicals*, ed. W.J. Gibbons (New York: Paulist Press, 1963), p. 147.

[14] *Laborem exercens*, n. 8, G. Baum, *The Priority of Labor*, p. 110.

[15] Cf. Nicole Laurin Frenette, *Recherches sociographiques*, 21 (1980): 151-162.

[16] See Jacques Grand'Maison, *Nouveaux modèles sociaux et développement* (Montreal: Hurtubise, 1971), especially pp. 460-462, and *Des milieux de travail* (Montreal: Les Presses de L'Université de Montréal, 1975).

Chapter Five
Douglas Hall: Contextual Theology

[1] Douglas Hall, *Thinking the Faith: Christian Theology in a North American Context* (Minneapolis: Augsburg, 1989). An incomplete list of D. Hall's books: *The Reality of the Gospel and the Unreality of the Churches* (Philadelphia: Westminster Press, 1972); *Lighten Our Darkness: Toward an Indigenous Theology of the Cross* (Philadelphia: Westminster Press, 1976); *The Canada Crisis: A Christian Perspective* (Toronto: Anglican Book Centre, 1980); *The Stewardship of Life and the Kingdom of Death* (New York: Friendship Press, 1985); *God and Human Suffering* (Grand Rapids: Eerdmans, 1986); *The Future of the Church* (Toronto: United Church Publishing House, 1989).

[2] See especially Douglas Hall, *Lighten Our Darkness* (Philadelphia: Westminster Press, 1976); also *Thinking the Faith*, pp. 22-33.

[3] *Thinking the Faith*, pp. 111-126, 148-152, 326-332.

[4] *Ibid.*, pp. 158-164.

[5] *Ibid.*, pp. 164-169.

[6] *Ibid.*, pp. 18, 42.

[7] *Ibid.*, p. 319.

[8] George Grant, *Lament for a Nation: The Defeat of Canadian Nationalism* (Toronto: Mclelland and Stewart, 1965).

[9] Douglas Hall, *The Canada Crisis* (Toronto: Anglican Book Centre, 1980), pp. 82-85.

[10] Cf. *The Ecumenist* 15 (September-October): 85-86.

[11] *Thinking the Faith*, p. 142.

[12] *Ibid.*, pp. 390-399.

Chapter Six
Ethical Reflections
on the Quebec Language Debate

[1] *La Justice sociale comme bonne nouvelle, Messages sociaux, économiques et politiques des évêques du Québec, 1972-83* (Montreal: Bellarmin, 1984), pp. 111-118.

[2] "The Universal Declaration of Human Rights," in *The Human Rights Reader,* ed. Walter Laqueur (New York: New American Library, 1990), pp. 197-202.

[3] "Ethical Reflections on the Economic Crisis," G. Baum and D. Cameron, *Ethics and Economics* (Toronto: Lorimer, 1984), pp. 3-18.

[4] *The Human Rights Reader,* p. 216.

[5] See pp. 161-162 of this book.

[6] See pp. 21-24 of this book.

[7] *Canadian Journal of Political and Social Theory* 6 (Winter, Spring 1982): 139-142.

[8] *The McGill Reporter,* 18 January 1989, p. 3.

[9] *Ibid.,* p. 5.

Chapter Seven
The Bishops and Quebec Nationalism

[1] See, in this book, chapter 1.

[2] See, in this book, chapter 2.

[3] *Do Justice! The Social Teaching of the Canadian Catholic Bishops,* E.F. Sheridan, ed. (Toronto: Jesuit Centre for Social Faith and Justice, 1987), pp. 399-410.

[4] See this book, pp. 31-33.

[5] *Do Justice!* pp. 122-134.

[6] *Do Justice!* p. 126.

[7] *La justice sociale comme bonne nouvelle: Messages sociaux, économiques et politiques des évêques du Québec: 1972-1983* (Montreal: Éditions Bellarmin, 1984), pp. 137-145.

[8] *Ibid.,* pp. 110-118, 114.

[9] *Ibid.,* p. 139. (English translation by G. Baum.)

[10] *Ibid.*

[11]   *Ibid.*, p. 112.

[12]   *Ibid.*, p. 113.

[13]   *Ibid.*, p. 114.

[14]   *Ibid.*, p. 115.

[15]   *L'Église de Montréal,* February 16, 1989, p. 151.

[16]   *Do Justice!* p. 332.

[17]   *La justice sociale comme bonne nouvelle,* pp. 157-166.

[18]   *Ibid.*

[19]   *Ibid.*, pp. 145-156.

[20]   Paul Tillich, *The Socialist Decision* (New York: Harper & Row, 1977). Original publication, 1932. Because of his severe criticism of the nationalism fostered by the Nazi party, Tillich had to leave Germany after the Nazi take-over in January 1933.

Index of Names

Achevé d'imprimer
en mai 1991 sur les presses
des Ateliers Graphiques Marc Veilleux Inc.
Cap-Saint-Ignace, Qué.